A NATIONAL HISTORIC
LANDMARK

"This site possesses national significance in commemorating the history of the U.S.A." These are the words engraved on the National Historic Landmark plaque, dedicated in 1977, and located in the Garden Patio of the Hotel del Coronado.

Indeed, this legendary grandame of the Pacific Ocean is one of our most prized historic possessions, erected during a time when President Grover Cleveland was in the White House and Wyatt Earp was in Tombstone. The architects of this now world-renowned structure had built only railroad stations and trestles before taking on the mammoth task of designing and creating a resort which quickly became "the talk of the Western world."

After eleven months of around-the-clock construction, the Hotel del Coronado opened to a host of curious spectators on February 19, 1888. Thus began a grand procession of visitors, including 12 U.S. presidents, a host of foreign leaders, well-known celebrities, international travelers, as well as neighbors from communities nearby. They all come to find a room for a night or two and more importantly, to experience an atmosphere of mystique, elegance and culture which has been all but lost in the march of time and progress.

In addition to being a National Historic Landmark, the Hotel del Coronado is Number 844 on the California Landmark registry, it is a San Diego County Historical Landmark, a Coronado Historic Landmark and is listed in the National Register of Historical Places.

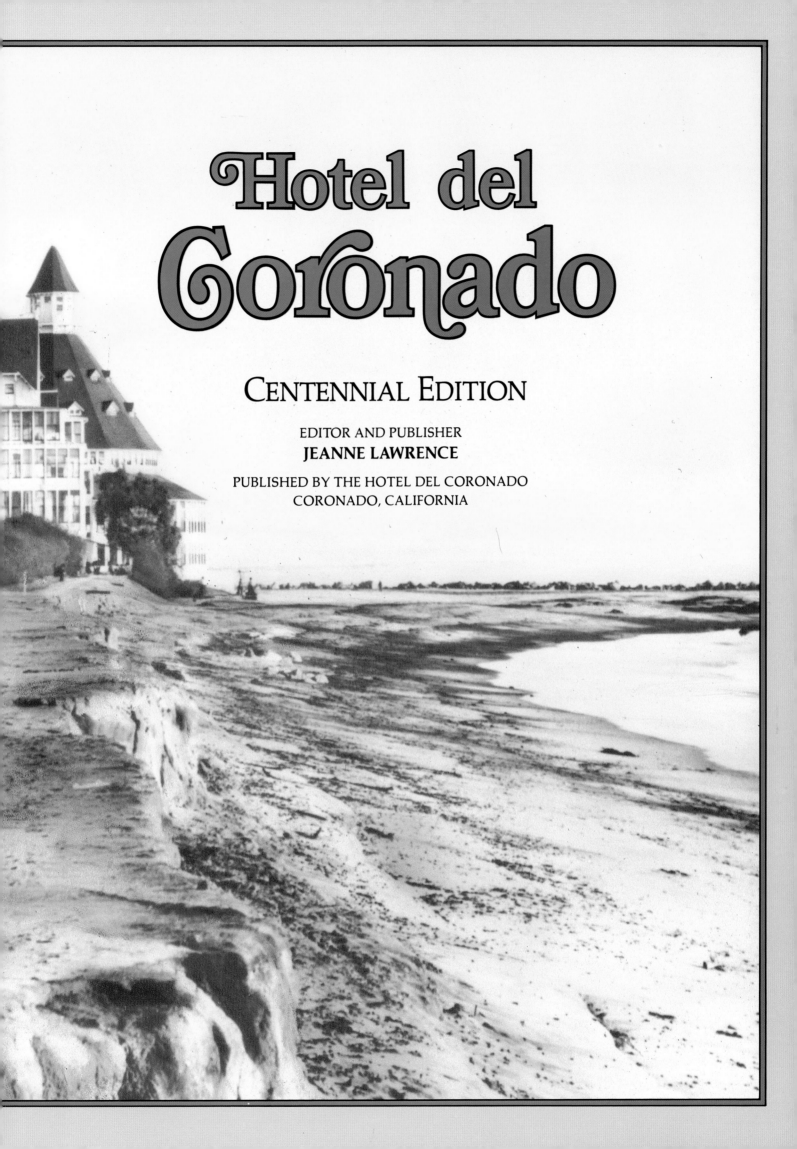

Hotel del Coronado

CENTENNIAL EDITION

EDITOR AND PUBLISHER
JEANNE LAWRENCE

PUBLISHED BY THE HOTEL DEL CORONADO
CORONADO, CALIFORNIA

Wealthy hotel patrons of the 1890s were afforded a special rail spur up the Silver Strand for their private cars, allowing them to park virtually at the front door of the famed Hotel del Coronado. The spur had been built by the owners during construction to bring building supplies and materials from the mainland.

PHOTO CREDITS

San Diego Historical Society: front flap, inside front cover insets,
4, 8, 10, 11, 12, 13, 14, 15, 16, 17, 18, 22, 24, 28, 29, 30, 31, 32, 34, 40, 41, 44, 45, 48 right.

Hotel del Coronado: back cover, inside front cover,
14, 19, 21, 24, 27, 28, 31, 34, 38, 50, 53, 54, 58, 62 bottom, 66.

Tim Stahl: inside front cover insets, 14 lower left, 23, 26 top, lower left, 32 top, 39, 42,
46 lower, 47 lower, 52 right, lower left, 53, 55, 59, 63, 64 top, inside back cover, back flap.

Nick Karras: 48 left, 49, 52 left, 62 top.

Hara: Cover, 44, 45, 48, 56, 60.

Larry du Pont: 2, 36, 71.

Alan Decker: 27.

Tommy Lark: additional photos.

Copyright ©1984 by the Hotel del Coronado
1500 Orange Avenue
Coronado, California 92118
(619) 435-6611
This book, or parts thereof, must not be reproduced in any form without permission.

SEQUOIA
COMMUNICATIONS

Produced for the Hotel del Coronado by Sequoia Communications
Design by Margo Chase   Printed in Japan   ISBN 0-917859-02-2

Third Printing, 1988

ACKNOWLEDGMENTS

A special thanks goes out to Tom Morrow, whose able direction enabled this publication to become a reality.

Valuable assistance in the writing of this book was given by a large numbers of quarters, including the San Diego Public Library, the San Diego Historical Society, the San Diego Union, the Title Insurance Company, the Coronado Historical Association, and many staff members of the Hotel del Coronado.

Invaluable contributions were made by hotel designer Dixon Morrow, who provided significant historical details on the hotel's interior and structure; hotel carpenter Mark Andrews, who makes it his job to know all the attics and cupolas throughout the massive wooden structure; personnel director Mike Caputa, who furnished background on past and present hotel staff members; hotel historian Steve Oakford, who is a walking volume of significant historical data; Don Larson, hotel director of marketing and advertising, Judith Bond and Marcie Buckley, who all gave valuable assistance and direction in finding specific research information; and long-time staff members Les Webb, Bud O'Brien and George Chapman who shared their memories and helped reconstruct the history of events over the past forty years. Without the assistance of these sources, this book would not have been possible.

The Hotel del Coronado is famous for its beautiful interior courtyard.

TABLE OF CONTENTS

HOTEL OF
VISIONARIES

The Hotel del Coronado has been in existence for 100 years, and yet, there have been only six owners. From Elisha Babcock, Jr., the first, to M. Larry Lawrence, the present, all have been men of vision, insight and energy.

In 1884, when Babcock was thirty-six, he came to San Diego from Evansville, Indiana with his wife, Isabel, and their sons. He had been a railroad executive, forced into early retirement because of poor health. Though San Diego was little more than a sleepy port, Babcock saw that the area had great potential as a place where people could go to escape from the harsh Eastern winters.

Babcock and his good friend, H. L. Story (of the Story and Clark Piano Company, Chicago), spent much time hunting on the wild Coronado peninsula, across the bay from San Diego. The only access was by boat, so the two hunters rowed more than a mile in order to reach the brush-covered jut of land in their search of jackrabbit, cottontail and quail. Looking out across the open sea, opposite flat, barren land, the two men began to dream of the possibilities offered by this unique stretch of real estate.

With the railroad promising soon to reach California's southernmost city and the United States' farthest corner, both Babcock and Story recognized an opportunity to lure people from all over the country to San Diego's wonderful climate, balmy Pacific breezes, quiet harbor and lush countryside. If Babcock and Story could enjoy this garden spot for hunting and fishing, then surely could those in the Eastern cities, who longed to travel West while still retaining some semblance of civilization, culture and comfort.

Some might want to settle in San Diego permanently. However, the two men recognized that, because of its remoteness and its lack of full services and communications, many simply would want to make the area a temporary destination for resting from the rigors of life in the big cities, and for escaping from the colder climates.

Babcock and Story began to ponder how best to take advantage of the opportunities that lay before them. The onslaught of travelers surely would come—and soon.

They formed a syndicate and called it the Coronado Beach Company. Its goal was to buy the peninsula and develop it into a city. From the profits of this enterprise, a magnificent resort hotel could be built, one that would attract visitors from around the world.

Ground-breaking ceremonies for The Del took place in 1887 (above). Born into an infant community with few services, the hotel had to be self-sufficient from the beginning. It had its own power plant, laundry facilities and foundry. Railroad and ferryboat systems were built to transport lumber, building materials, fixtures and furnishings, and of course, human cargo.

In 1885, when the first transcontinental railroad opened the way to Barstow in the Mojave Desert, some 150 miles north, the two men made their move. They purchased the entire Coronado peninsula for $110,000.

Services had to be provided if they were to attract any people at all to this flat land filled with little else but sagebrush. A pipeline was laid from San Diego's Old Town in order to bring water from the San Diego River. A transportation system of ferryboats, wharves and even steam engine trains was installed. The brush was cleared, streets were laid out and trees were planted. Electricity was virtually unknown in California, but foresight led the two men to build one of the state's first power plants. The plant would not only furnish power to their future hotel, but to the entire city of Coronado until 1922. Another new invention, the telephone, became a part of the planned community. And a railroad extension was planned that would run along the eastern harbor shore to the south end of the bay and up the thin peninsula known as the Silver Strand.

A promotional campaign was begun. A number of Eastern newspapers carried daily San Diego temperatures, which made it the only California city, other than San Francisco, to be so honored. Rand McNally, the Chicago-based publisher, put out a booklet which heralded the advantages of life in Coronado. Meanwhile, in Coronado, a pavilion was erected and regular parties were given in which wives Isabel Babcock and Della Story held court. On July 4, 1886, a great picnic celebration was held, beginning a Coronado tradition which continues to this day.

As interest developed in their planned community, the developers shifted their thoughts to the creation of a central theme for Coronado: a place where travelers could gather to relax, hunt, fish or even ponder an investment in the young community. Babcock said he wanted to create a hotel—a resort—which would become "the talk of the Western world."

Although Babcock and Story selected the Reid Brothers as architects for their wondrous dream resort, at least one designer was brought in to submit ideas before the former railroad architects arrived. Clinton Day's design was called "ornamental and striking" in a San Diego *Union* column (November 13, 1886), concluding that "the entire plan is one of beauty."

The same day the *Union* column appeared, some 6000 people (about half the population of San Diego) lined up for a free boat ride across the bay to the Coronado Beach Company's free picnic lunch, which also served as a pitch offering people a chance to invest in the new community. The terms were: one-third down, balance due in twelve months at ten percent interest. No discounts were given for cash. An ad announcing the land auction read:

> The object of the auction of Coronado Beach property is to make a basis for prices on the unsold portions. At the close of the auction, property having the same relative location will be advanced twenty-five percent above prices obtained at the auction. This positively assures a handsome profit on any investment...

Fortunately, it was a time of abundant money supply and no government regulations.

Prospective investors disembarked from boats at the northern tip of the peninsula (near the end of present-day Orange Avenue.) They boarded railroad cars and were taken for a slow look at what must have been a wondrous sight: the once-brush-covered hunters' paradise had been transformed into a genteel Eden. Markers indicated planned streets and green shrubs replaced the once dominant sagebrush.

Orange Avenue, which remains today the city's main thoroughfare, was laced down the center with a double row of orange trees. At Sixth Avenue, the trains slowed in order to show off the new town plaza. Passengers could see palms lining Palm Avenue and olive trees decorating Olive Avenue.

Brochures emphasized Coronado's climate and soil and its ability to grow exotic ornamental plants year-round as well as lush vegetable gardens. (The sales literature, however, failed to note that alcoholic beverages were forbidden in Coronado. The Hotel del Coronado, at the beginning anyway, had a monopoly on the sale of liquor.)

As the train neared the narrow spot of the peninsula, where the Silver Strand begins, passengers disembarked and crowded into a large tent for the promised free lunch and land auction. The lunch was adequate, but the auction was lively indeed.

An important part of Coronado's history returned in time for the 1988 centennial. Prior to the Hotel del Coronado's 100th anniversary, passengers were again able to enjoy the leisurely junket across San Diego Bay to and from the hotel, thanks to the return of the ferry service. Rubber-wheeled trolleys are also now available to transport guests to and from the ferry.

(Above): The first men of vision: E. S. Babcock, railroad man from Evansville, Illinois (far left); Alonzo Horton, father of new San Diego (white beard); and H. L. Story, piano magnate from Chicago (right).

(Right): Hotel—south front, 1924.

(Opposite): Elisha S. Babcock, c. 1900.

The day was a success, just as Babcock and Story had hoped. By 4 p.m., they had recouped their initial investment; they were on their way to amassing a huge profit which would be used to build their dream resort. The San Diego *Union* took note of the occasion:

> *The sale was highly satisfactory to the salesmen and to the owners and the prices brought far above what everyone had dared to fix as the limit. One shrewd real estate man said: "I expected to see those lots go for $200 on an average, but bless my stars, these prices just rattle me."*

The choice ocean-view lots went for as much as $1600 and, out of 285 properties sold on November 13 and 14, 1886, only twenty-two went for less than $200.

With enough money to begin serious planning and even construction, Babcock telegraphed the Reid Brothers, back in Evansville, Indiana; they were still working for the railroad from which Babcock had retired.

When James, Merritt and Watson Reid made their way West, they were reminded more than once that they were traveling through untamed America. (At one point, a sheriff's posse boarded the train, riding to the next town to capture a bandit.) They decided to take the final leg of their journey by sea.

After arriving, James Reid would later recall the brothers' first glimpse of Coronado: "The next day, such a one as may be found only in Coronado in December, we all visited the beach. No finer location could have been found anywhere."

Like hundreds of thousands of visitors who followed them, the Reid Brothers had no desire to leave. They looked upon the calm Pacific Ocean, the Coronado Islands (which lay offshore in Mexican waters), Point Loma and the entrance to beautiful San Diego Bay, the mountains behind San Diego and southeast to the quiet Glorietta Bay. How could a world-class resort be located in a more picturesque setting?

On January 12, 1887, a ground-breaking ceremony for the new hotel was held. Isabel Babcock turned the first shovel of dirt. (In 1938, James Reid recalled the ceremony as having taken place in March, but according to newspaper accounts in

the San Diego *Union*, the ground-breaking was in January and the laying of the foundation was in March.)

Materials and labor were scarce in San Diego at the time. A large contingent of unskilled Chinese laborers, along with master carpenters, plumbers and other craftsmen, were transported by boat from San Francisco and Oakland in order to work on the giant project. Anxious to complete the hotel as soon as possible, Babcock and his designers would have liked workers for day *and* night shifts, but finding workers for the day shift proved difficult enough. According to newspaper accounts, the labor union saw to it that its workers were on the job for only nine hours per day. To compensate, the unskilled Chinese laborers were trained on the job. Eventually, enough workers were found to man the construction site twenty-four hours per day.

Bricks were fired from a kiln, built nearby specifically for the construction project, and the San Diego Granite Company provided rock from quarries in Temecula Canyon.

When work began on the twelve-foot-high foundation in March, 1887, some 100 barrels of cement were poured daily.

In the meantime, china was ordered from Paris, glassware from Belgium, toilet seats from England and 21,000 yards of carpet were shipped from Lowell, Massachusetts. A Boston furniture maker designed and produced wooden chairs, christened "Coronado Diners."

Construction could not proceed fast enough. As the foundation went up, so did expectations and it was announced prematurely that the huge hotel would be ready by November. In September, a Mr. and Mrs. H. B. Wilkins made the hotel's first room reservations, actually selecting their room from the architects' plans. By October, a twenty-four-foot flag of blue silk was unfurled. However, it was soon obvious that construction would not meet the November target date. The opening was postponed until mid-December.

At the same time he was designing and building The Del, as the Hotel del Coronado has affectionately come to be known, James Reid was working on another hotel project in the infant community. The "Josephine," a smaller wooden

structure, would actually be finished ahead of the "big hotel." This was fortunate for some of the first guests of the big hotel, because when they arrived in mid-December, expecting to occupy their rooms in America's largest Pacific Coast resort, they found workmen scurrying to complete the project. Although the Josephine has long since been razed, it opened in the fall of 1887. No doubt it accommodated a good many disappointed guests who had traveled thousands of miles to be among the first to experience the dream resort by the sea.

The Josephine, which was later renamed the "Iturbitide," was built in the same Queen Anne style as its larger counterpart on the beach. It had a tall tower and shingled cupola and similar wood turnings. Like the Hotel del Coronado, the Josephine had electricity, receiving power from Babcock's new power plant on The Del property. (The power plant structure, complete with smokestack, can be seen today along the east driveway entrance to the resort. It serves as the print shop and communications office for the hotel.)

Furniture started arriving at the hotel's unfinished structure in November, 1887, followed, in December, by the first members of the staff. Because the project was behind schedule, pressures mounted for the hotel's first manager, John B. Seghers, who was also called upon to act as the hotel's first decorator!

(Above): John D. Spreckels built the pier pictured above in the early 1900s. It was destroyed in 1906 by a huge tidal wave.

(Below): Early hotel laundry delivery vehicle. The Hotel del Coronado has always had its own laundry facilities. Today, in addition to providing service to the hotel, it also services some twenty nearby hotels and motels.

(Opposite): Early woodworking tools used in the hotel's construction.

The San Diego *Union* recorded an "informal" opening of the hotel on February 1, 1888, with the promise of a "formal" opening in the near future. At this time, the Nelson Morris party from Chicago moved *en suite* into rooms 138 and 141, and became the first official guests to put their names on the hotel's register. In the following days, they were joined by guests from across the nation, including those from Kansas City, St. Louis, San Francisco, Minneapolis, Cheyenne, Omaha, Boston, Washington, D.C. and New York City.

On February 19, the hotel served its first meals; this was some three weeks after the first guests had checked in. Construction continued for the next several months. However, the inconvenience didn't stop people from flocking to this unusual Victorian seaside resort which mirrored those of Brighton along the southern English coastline.

Those first meals were served in what was simply called "the dining room"

In the early 1890s, the hotel's sun porches also served as entry ways to rooms as there were no hallways as they exist today.

(now known as the Crown Room), and it is one of America's monumental architectural achievements. Stretching 156 feet long, sixty-six feet wide and rising thirty-three feet high, the magnificent sugar pine-paneled ceiling was hand-fitted without a single nail. It remains one of the nation's largest support-free rooms.

The U.S. economy had been strong when construction began in 1887, but it soured and fell on hard times as the hotel neared completion; this probably explains the delay of the grand opening. The economic downturn sent people away from San Diego—and back to their homes—as quickly as they had come.

As Babcock and Story were realizing their dream, yet another vision had begun to take shape. John D. Spreckels sailed into the quiet San Diego harbor in July of 1887. The son of "sugar king" Claus Spreckels (he imported sugar from Hawaii to San Francisco), John was determined to make his own mark in the world. He quickly fell in love with the sleepy port in spite, or perhaps because of its many needs. One of his first ventures was to build a coal bunker and a wharf that would service the area's railroad trains. He thus assured their valuable continued presence.

Over the next forty years, Spreckels would join San Diego's other pioneers, such as Alonzo Horton, Babcock, and Story, in helping to create a modern city. By far, Spreckels was the wealthiest of them all. He built a streetcar system, bought and published the two leading newspapers, the *Union* and the *Tribune*, developed real estate, became a banker, brought in much-needed water from the mountains and, in a project that nearly ruined him financially, Spreckels built the San Diego, Arizona and Eastern Railway. This system went around and through the steep mountains east of the city and linked the desert and mountain communities to San Diego.

Almost from his first day in San Diego, Spreckels was intrigued by the development of Coronado and by the fascinating structure which dominated the horizon of the flat land plate across the bay. Babcock, who had run into financial difficulties, successfully convinced Spreckels to invest in the Coronado Beach Company. As the years passed, Spreckels' involvement grew. By the turn of the century, Spreckels was running the company and hotel from his home in San Francisco; Babcock had become just another employee on the payroll.

(Opposite top): Construction was begun in March, 1887, and the hotel opened just eleven months later!

(Opposite bottom): J. D. Spreckels as a young man.

(Left): The U.S. Navy began using the beaches near the Hotel del Coronado to train in the early 1900s, during the days of the Great White Fleet. Today, the nearby Naval installations still use the beach areas near the famed resort for physical fitness and swim training.

(Below): Heavyweight champion Jack Dempsey was a frequent visitor to the Hotel.

(Bottom): Among the famous heroes visiting The Del was baseball great Babe Ruth (on left).

Prior to the arrival of the Spreckels family at the hotel in 1906, The Del was closed from June until December of 1902, for renovation and completion of some unfinished work. It was during this time that the famed Tent City emerged to the south along the Silver Strand.

Much of Coronado's social life centered around Tent City, according to hotel historian Stephen S. Oakford. It had the beach, boating activities and an indoor saltwater plunge. It offered concerts, plays and vaudeville shows. Local residents as well as hotel guests flocked to these performances. Tent City flourished as one of the country's most popular vacation spots until, sadly, its closure in 1939.

The San Francisco earthquake of 1906 was all it took to convince Spreckels to make San Diego his permanent home. He loaded his family and belongings aboard his yacht, *Lurline*, and brought them south to the Hotel del Coronado. They would live at the hotel until their splendid granite mansion was built across the street. (This mansion can be seen today as the Glorietta Bay Inn.)

Spreckels guided the hotel through one of its most opulent periods. During this era, The Del was visited by several U.S. presidents. In 1909, it hosted San Diego's first Charity Ball. And the most famous state visit of all, that of His Royal Highness, the Prince of Wales, took place in 1920.

When Spreckels died in 1927, his successors faced serious problems. There were matters of succession within the companies that controlled his holdings. (He had invested heavily in a decaying streetcar system; the once-popular public transportation system was gradually being replaced by the private automobile.)

In later years, when the Great Depression hit, the Spreckels family sold some properties, held onto others. The Hotel del Coronado was kept in the portfolio. It did not officially go up for sale until after World War II. The years had taken their toll and The Del was no longer the well-polished resort it had once been. The grand visits of Eastern and Hollywood elite had all but ceased, while the hotel was burdened by some 100 permanent guests who lived in it on the American Plan (meals included) at a low rate.

A strange and little-known transaction took place in 1948, which conveyed

(Above): The first of many presidents to visit The Del—Benjamin Harrison, 1891.

(Below): An exciting event at The Del ballroom, 1924.

ownership of the Hotel del Coronado to Robert A. Nordblom and a small group of investors. However, prominent Kansas City hotelier Barney Goodman became the hotel's fourth owner only two days later.

Goodman had the vision and the business sense to begin restoring the old hotel to the prominence it previously enjoyed. The permanent guests were asked to leave, a fifth floor was added along with another fifty rooms. Goodman renovated existing rooms and improved both the outward and inward appearance with much-needed paint.

Unfortunately, Goodman's untimely death in 1951 curtailed the hotel's complete renovation. The hotel was held in trust for his two sons until 1960, but the impetus for renovation died when Goodman did.

San Diego businessman John S. Alessio became the hotel's fifth owner in 1960. Alessio immediately set upon a new renovation and improvement program. Public areas and guest rooms were his targets as he spent millions of dollars on the project. It was Alessio who had the Grand Ballroom's high ceiling lowered to allow for better sound control. The original narrow windows of the Crown and Coronet rooms were removed and replaced with the huge plate glass windows of today.

The Hotel del Coronado Corporation purchased the hotel from Alessio in 1963, again, before renovation was fully realized. M. Larry Lawrence, chairman of the board, serves as the hotel's sixth owner, directing day-to-day operations. The Lawrence Plan has been to restore the hotel to its Victorian splendor and charm, and retain its attraction as a pleasure spot and as a scene for San Diego social events. Lawrence is also expanding the hotel's appeal as a resort and convention center.

A continuous renovation program was instituted by Lawrence's designer, Dixon Morrow. This program has no less than five rooms out of service at all times for redecoration and upgrading, and paint crews constantly keep this grand old lady dressed in her best white.

M. LARRY LAWRENCE

One of Southern California's most successful developers and entrepreneurs is Chicago-born M. Larry Lawrence. After serving in World War II as a merchant marine, Lawrence attended the University of Arizona where he became a football hero. He returned to his native Chicago after college and entered several different professions: he was a partner in a public relations firm, an active real estate broker, a general contractor and an insurance broker. During this period, in the 1940s and early '50s, he developed more than $60 million in construction projects.

He moved his family to California in 1953. There he continued his general contracting and insurance businesses and added securities to his list of activities. Since moving to California, he has been responsible for more than $300 million in residential and commercial projects.

He is noted for his wide range of philanthropic projects as well as for a variety of civic works. Lawrence is well known on a national scale for his political activities. He is also a member of the Federal Home Loan Bank board.

His first love, however, is his grand lady by the Pacific—the Hotel del Coronado—which he has guided carefully through a period of renaissance since 1963. As chairman of the board of the Hotel del Coronado Corporation, he has faced some tough decisions over the years; the first was whether or not to invest millions of dollars in order to bring The Del back to her original state of elegance and beauty.

"I felt we would have to do some serious renovation to justify the hotel's continued existence," he said in an interview. As a developer, his experience with architecture and engineering dictated quite clearly what had to be done to make the hotel functional. When his organization took control of the hotel, its mechanical and electrical elements didn't work. The plumbing was in such bad shape that little, if any, water pressure went beyond the third floor, and in some areas, there was no water at all. Other areas simply had no hot water. It was clear to Lawrence that these things had to be rectified immediately or authorities would certainly condemn portions of and possibly the entire hotel, thereby forcing its closure.

Between 1963 and 1988, $80 million was spent restoring, repairing and replacing those systems least noticed by the public. Mechanical, plumbing, electrical, heating, ventilation, and cooking gas lines were improved and a myriad of structural work was done just to keep the hotel alive.

Lawrence was concerned with fire and safety codes. Measures were taken that exceeded the requirements, giving the Hotel del Coronado one of the best fire ratings of any building in the world. This is a point of special pride to Lawrence because The Del is the world's largest wooden structure. The hotel's Grinnell sprinkler system is one of the finest, most expensive of its kind and provides guests the utmost in fire safety. "You'll float away before you even smell smoke," quips Lawrence.

Lawrence correctly gambled on making the Hotel del Coronado one of Southern California's largest and most successful meeting and convention facilities. He constructed the Grande Hall with a meeting capacity of 1500, thereby increasing the hotel's ability to accommodate large groups. The hotel has expanded from 399 to 700 rooms due to the addition of the seven-floor Ocean Towers complex and the poolside complex.

But these new facilities were not created at the expense of the Reid Brothers' fragile architecture of nearly a century ago. Lawrence brought in the best designers so the newer complexes blended skillfully and beautifully with the main building, maintaining the hotel's familiar white body and bright red roof trademark.

Lawrence is highly respected for his self-made financial success, but no accomplishment is more dear to him than his restoration of one of the world's most beautiful man-made historic landmarks—the grandame of American seaside resorts—the Hotel del Coronado.

CONSTRUCTING A LEGEND

The Hotel del Coronado is generally considered to be the last remaining extravagantly-conceived seaside resort. She stands as a monument to the past with her red-roofed turrets, intricate woodwork, handcrafted pillars and ornate Victorian gingerbread. For nearly a century, The Del has set a standard by which other resorts are measured, and as the years go by, this leadership continues to grow. Today, guests at The Del enjoy a spectrum of conveniences and recreational facilities which are rare among resorts of the Western world. San Diego County is California's third most populated county while San Diego is the state's second largest city. But little more than a century ago, there were less than 250,000 people in the entire state and only about 25,000 in all of Southern California. No one in his wildest dreams could have imagined such growth!

In 1846, Don Pedro Carrillo acquired the 4100-acre piece of real estate via a Spanish land grant. At that time, the Coronado peninsula was scrubs and weeds which fed the jackrabbits and coyotes. (Movie and television buffs will be interested to know that Carrillo was the grandfather of popular actor Leo Carrillo, who was best known as the Cisco Kid's sidekick, Pancho.) Don Pedro sold the land in 1849, after Mexico ceded California to the United States, for the total sum of $1000, or 25 cents an acre.

By 1869, after the end of the Civil War, the 4100 acres of Coronado peninsula were purchased for $10,000. In December, 1885, Elisha Babcock and H. L. Story bought the entire peninsula for $110,000—this is more than 100 times what Don Pedro had sold it for! Babcock and Story promoted the sale of the land offered by their Coronado Beach Company in a number of ways. Their first promotion was their "Name-the-City" contest which offered a cash prize to the winning name. "Coronado" was taken from the offshore island chain that lies south in Mexican waters. (These four small islands were named in 1542 by Juan Rodriguez Cabrillo, a Portuguese navigator in the service of the king of Spain. Cabrillo was the first European to sail into San Diego Bay.)

The land company was successfully selling parcels for the new community of Coronado. So, Babcock brought the three Reid Brothers, James, Merritt and Watson, to the peninsula in 1886, to design for him a hotel that would become "the talk of the Western world!" Essentially, this is all the Reids had to work with. The results were almost identical to Babcock's visionary description. It was built for $1 million—$600,000 for the structure and $400,000 for the furnishings.

When the hotel was constructed, there were no other facilities on the peninsula and only basic

ones were available in San Diego. The Reids had to build the workshops needed for constructing the huge structure. Included in these workshops were a brick kiln, a metal shop, a foundry and a planing mill. The mill was needed because all of the wood was rough cut and much of it was green and in need of finishing. All of the necessary bricks were prepared at the hotel's "Brickyard Cove," a sizable deposit of good brick clay on the Silver Strand (also known as the sandpit in those early days). Tons of brick were required for the foundations, fireplaces and chimneys. The clay was dug out, mixed with water and sun-dried in wooden molds, then fired in nearby kilns. When the kilns cooled, the bricks were trundled onto a short wharf where they were loaded aboard scows and towed by San Diego Bay's first steam vessel, the tugboat *Emma*, into Glorietta Bay. Enough laborers and carpenters skilled to work on the mammoth project were difficult to find. This may have been because much of the work required was at great heights. (The main tower, which covers the Grand Ballroom, would rise nearly ten stories, an unheard of height in those days.) It was considered dangerous because much of the construction had to be accomplished by simple ladder-climbing and rope-and-pulley methods. The going wage in 1887 was $2.50 to $3 per day for a sixty-hour work week. To complicate matters, final drawings were not complete and details were left to craftsmen on the job. In many cases, the Reids' design work was only a day or two ahead of the construction!

Many workers were brought down by boat from San Francisco; most of these were unskilled Chinese laborers who had to be trained on the job. The entire 2000-man crew worked around the clock, using the Reids' preliminary drawings as their primary guidelines. Work was begun in March, 1887, and on February 19, 1888, scarcely eleven months later, the first guests were officially welcomed into the hotel. Some 324 staff members, including porters, chambermaids, gardeners, waiters and chefs, had to be transported from the East Coast prior to the opening.

The present owner, M. Larry Lawrence, has spent the past twenty-five years—and more than $80 million—in restoring, renovating and ensuring that the original state of the property is maintained and preserved. Yet, he also works hard to keep the hotel's facilities up-to-date. Originally, nearly every room had a fireplace, though all except one have been replaced by bathrooms. Each room had its own wall safe, a luxury which has been reinstituted. Other behind-the-scenes amenities have remained through the years and today guests will still find hotel butcher and pastry shops, a bake shop, upholstery and furniture shops, electric and plumbing shops, machine shops and a laundry. These facilities were all built when the hotel was constructed, to support the workmen and finally the guests of the Hotel del Coronado.

STARSTRUCK

AT THE DEL

Over the years, more celebrities of the arts, entertainment and sports worlds have visited the Hotel del Coronado than any other hotel resort in North America. Add to this the countless local celebrations—either to raise money or a little bit of hell—and you have one of the world's truly great places where the famous relax, hide from or mingle with everyday travelers; and they do it amid the luxury and elegance that was once the style and grace of Europe's elite.

Countless tales exist—some true, some legendary and some nearly forgotten—of the notables who have experienced The Del. One such story is recalled by Carleton Lichty, former vice-chairman of the corporate board.

"Jimmy Doolittle, the famed Army aviator, told this story on himself," recalls Lichty. "General Doolittle and his wife lived in a little house in Coronado during the 1920s when Doolittle was a second lieutenant stationed at Rockwell Field (now known as North Island Naval Air Station). The Doolittles dreamed of staying at The Del. They saved their money, and finally had enough to check in and enjoy the honeymoon they never had. The problem was, according to the general, they didn't have enough money to buy food at the hotel, or so they thought. They ate at a greasy spoon restaurant some blocks away from the hotel, and it wasn't until they checked out that the couple discovered the hotel was on the American Plan, meaning that meals were included in the price of the room."

Lichty, one of the nation's most respected hoteliers, was in charge of managing The Del on two different occasions, first during John Alessio's tenure as owner and returning in 1965 under Larry Lawrence. Like managers before him, Lichty saw his share of celebrities, presidents and foreign dignitaries. The largest state dinner ever held at the hotel was in 1970, when President Richard Nixon hosted Mexican President Gustavo Diaz Ordaz in the Crown Room, site of many other dinners over the years.

President Nixon selected the Hotel del Coronado because of his strong interest in history, and because he knew there was no dining room in America that equaled the Crown Room in scale, aesthetic beauty and social grace. It was an ideal setting for the pomp and ceremony Nixon felt was necessary for his Mexican counterpart. For San

*Celebrities and the politically lofty
frequent the Hotel del Coronado.
President Ronald Reagan, (below),
hosting a mini-conference at the hotel
in 1982. Vice President George Bush,
(right), is challenged to a game of tennis
by hotel general manager Scott Anderson
(in visor). Tennis star Chris Evert,
(middle left), playing on one of The Del's
championship courts. The TV series,
"Hart to Hart," (bottom left, taping
a segment at The Del in 1983.*

Diegans, it was a once-in-a-lifetime pageant, a chance to indulge personally in the
sort of elaborate state ceremony which citizens outside Washington, D.C., rarely
have the opportunity to see. More than 1000 invited guests attended the gala dinner,
including former President Lyndon B. Johnson and his wife Lady Bird, Secretary of
State William Rogers, Attorney General John Mitchell, General of the Army Omar
Bradley, California Governor Ronald Reagan and his wife Nancy, presidential aides
Henry Kissinger, H. R. Haldeman, Ronald Ziegler, and seven U.S. senators,
including Arizona's Barry Goldwater. And the event was not limited to politicians:
the late John Wayne headed an all-star Hollywood cast that included Frank Sinatra,
Art Linkletter, Red Skelton and Cesar Romero. Lichty recalls the evening as "one of
the most dramatic and elegant in all the rich history of the Hotel del Coronado."

Over the years, The Del has hosted twelve U.S. presidents, beginning with
Benjamin Harrison in April, 1891. In the years to follow, the hotel would
welcome presidents including William McKinley, William Howard Taft,
Woodrow Wilson, Franklin D. Roosevelt (who visited on a number of occasions
before and during his presidency), Dwight D. Eisenhower, John F. Kennedy, Richard
M. Nixon, Jimmy Carter, and most recently, President Ronald Reagan. (In October
of 1982, President Reagan hosted a mini-summit conference for Mexican President
Miguel de la Madrid; it was held in suite 3253 followed by lunch in the Coronet
Room. The beautifully-appointed suite, which overlooks the Pacific, has been
named the "Summit Suite" in honor of the occasion and displays photographs of the
historic session between the two neighboring heads of state.)

President Reagan is no stranger to The Del, which is one of his favorite
retreats. He has been a guest on numerous occasions, first while he was an actor,
then as governor of California and later as president. Suite 3119, the largest in the
main building, was named the "Governor's Suite" in Reagan's honor. He and Mrs.
Reagan stayed in this suite during this tenure as the California chief executive.
They loved the decor, the spacious design and the fact that it is the only guest
accommodation in the hotel with a private outside entrance.

According to the San Diego *Union*, less auspicious political guests have also

"SAIL AMERICA"

Over the years, the Hotel del Coronado has hosted hundreds of benefits to aid charitable organizations. In addition to providing the setting for these affairs, the management of the hotel has been personally involved in fund raising for these groups. On February 19, 1986, the Hotel del Coronado celebrated its 98th birthday with a benefit dinner for Sail America, the non-profit organization backing Skipper Dennis Conner's successful bid to regain the America's Cup. At that function, hotel owner M. Larry Lawrence, through the Hotel del Coronado affiliate Ocean Systems Research, Ltd., announced the donation of two yachts to Sail America's cause. The vessels, which had a combined value of $1.5 million, were the first yachts to be donated to Sail America's Yacht Donation Program, chaired by Mr. Lawrence. The dinner featured celebrity entertainment and the ceremonial exchange of keys to the yachts between Mr. Lawrence and Mr. Conner. Approximately $100 thousand was raised during this benefit, another in a series hosted by the hotel.

(Above): Skipper Dennis Conner and the Hotel Del's Larry Lawrence exchange keys to the Sail America yachts.

(Below): Pre-dinner reception guests at the Sail America benefit included (from left) Larry and Jeanne Lawrence, television celebrities Gregory Harison, Abby Dalton and Richard Mulligan, and Dennis Conner.

(Left): Ramon Navarro and Anita Page in a scene from The Flying Fleet, which was the first of many movies to be filmed in full or in part at The Del.

(Right): Margarita Fisher, actress of the silent screen and San Diego girl. Married to Harry Pollard, director of Pollard Film Play Company, she starred in Pearl of Paradise (1915), thought to have been shot at the Lubin Studios in Coronado.

L. Frank Baum's fabled Land of Oz bears a striking resemblance to The Del's well known conical spires. Baum visited the hotel many times in the early 1900s and eventually settled in Coronado.

stayed at The Del: Vice President Stevenson in 1893, the widow of John Jay Knox in 1895, Robert Todd Lincoln, son of the late president, in 1896 and Montgomery Ward in 1900.

During the hotel's construction in 1887, the world's most famous inventor, who had more than 1000 patents in his name when he died, personally supervised the installation of his incandescent lighting system. Thomas Alva Edison returned to the hotel in 1904, to throw the switch on The Del's first Christmas tree, a star pine which still stands on the front lawn at the east end of the Crown Room. Edison again returned to San Diego in 1915, for the Pan-American Exposition. This time he arrived with good friends Harvey Firestone and Henry Ford. They came at the invitation of G. Aubrey Davidson, who made The Del his permanent home.

World-famous New York publisher Joseph Pulitzer made headlines along the California coast because he was among The Del's first guests when it opened in February, 1888. Charles Nordhoff, a popular political writer of the day, was a guest in December, 1890. (His grandson, Charles Nordhoff, co-authored the best-selling classic, Mutiny on the Bounty in later years.)

Over the years, writers have been attracted to The Del. The hotel has charm and elegance, and maintains a mystique that fires the imagination; no doubt these characteristics have inspired a great many literary efforts. L. Frank Baum wrote books for his Wizard of Oz series at the hotel. His first visits were as a glassware salesman, later as a writer of these children's stories. He and his wife spent a month at a time at The Del, simply ingesting the peaceful setting which inspired him to design the chandeliers now hanging from the Crown Room restaurant ceiling. Illustrations in the Oz books show a marked similarity between his architectural fantasies and the hotel, and movie-watchers may note the Emerald City castle in the film version of The Wizard of Oz was also based on The Del's Victorian style. And, author Henry James managed to work in a two-day stay at the hotel in 1905, while traveling from his home in the East to a speaking engagement in Los Angeles.

Hollywood first discovered The Del in 1927, when it was selected as a location site for the Metro-Goldwyn-Mayer silent production of The Flying Fleet, which starred Ramon Navarro and a beautiful blond actress named Anita Page. (A young and talented actress, Miss Page later starred in Broadway Melody, the first musical to

(Above): Edward, Prince of Wales at a reception dinner in his honor, 1920. From left to right: Mrs. J. E. Kuhne, Governor William Stevens, Ellis Spreckels, the Prince of Wales, Mrs. Wilde (wife of mayor of San Diego). What were the prince and Ellis Spreckels discussing so intently? According to social columnist Eileen Jackson, "Hollywood, the movies, and all the glamour gals of those days."

CLOVER CLUB COCKTAIL

As described earlier, the royal visit by Britain's Prince of Wales in 1920, was a memorable one; people are still talking about it. A small episode, when the prince unexpectedly walked from the hotel to the nearby home of Claus Spreckels at 1043 Ocean Boulevard, resulted in the documentation of a tasty cocktail that was served to the prince. Ellis Spreckels, owner John Spreckels' daughter-in-law, had played an important part in arranging the royal visit. The prince wanted to personally pay his respects and thank her for all of her hard work. When he arrived, Mrs. Spreckels was just returning from the beach with her children and was naturally caught by surprise. After quickly getting out of her beach attire, the hostess and her daughters came downstairs to greet the royal visitor. There, Mrs. Spreckels served what she called the "Clover Club Cocktail."

The recipe for this royal concoction is as follows:

Juice from 1 lemon	2 tsp of grenadine
White of 1 egg	1 jigger of dry gin

Blend over cracked ice and strain.

win an Academy Award for Best Picture.) Miss Page adopted Coronado as her Shangri-la. After retiring, at the age of 26, she married a U.S. Naval officer and still lives within a mile of the hotel.

During the turbulent 1920s and '30s, The Del attracted many other Hollywood celebrities. Some of the more glamorous names included Mary Pickford, Tallulah Bankhead and Greta Garbo. Mae West was a guest in 1934. Charlie Chaplin was a regular member of Coronado's polo crowd which made the hotel its headquarters. And Sarah Bernhardt, the grand lady of American theater, found the hotel "charmante."

When movie companies come to the San Diego area, more often than not, they select the Hotel del Coronado as their prime location site. In 1972, the hotel became the background for "Ghost Story," a television series starring the late Sebastian Cabot. It didn't fare well in the ratings and was soon dropped by the network. Nevertheless, the Victorian architecture of The Del served well to create the required atmosphere. Other movies made over the years include *Loving Couples*, with Shirley MacLaine, *Wicked, Wicked*, a forgettable horror story, and *$*, with Goldie Hawn. Television movies filmed in part at the hotel have included: *The Girl, the Gold Watch and Everything; Captains and Kings;* and *Rich Man, Poor Man*. Television series such as "Hart to Hart," with Robert Wagner, and "Simon & Simon," with Jamieson Parker and Gerald McRaney, *Lifestyles of the Rich and Famous* and countless television commercials, have also used The Del.

The Del was the subject of a recent Hollywood film, but due to production difficulties, it was shot at another hotel. In 1975, Richard Matheson, who worked with Rod Serling on the popular "Twilight Zone" series, wrote a novel titled *Bid Time Return*. It is an enchanting story that takes the protagonist back through time to 1896; it is set entirely at the Hotel del Coronado. The book was made into a motion picture titled *Somewhere in Time*.

(Opposite): Children practicing diving at Tent City, c. 1920. Tent City was the center of many Coronado social activities until its closure in 1939.

(Above): Interior of bathhouse, 1890. The building, located a few blocks east of the hotel, served numerous bathers until it was demolished around 1930.

(Below): Actress Esther Williams and family, c. 1950s.

(Above): Stars attended a gala and exchanged awards on the 25th anniversary, in 1984, of filming the movie **Some Like It Hot.** *From left, director Billy Wilder, Jack Lemmon and Tony Curtis.*

(Opposite): Marilyn Monroe and Jack Lemmon, on location at The Hotel del Coronado for the 1958 filming of **Some Like It Hot,** *stroll, in costume, along the beach.*

(Below): Marilyn Monroe sizzles with **Some Like It Hot** *co-star Tony Curtis.*

The list of movies made at the Hotel del Coronado is a long one. But *Some Like It Hot* elicits the warmest and most affectionate smiles from the faces of long-time staff members. Filmed in part at the resort in 1958, it starred Marilyn Monroe, Jack Lemmon and Tony Curtis and was directed by Billy Wilder. Over the years, the film has gathered a cult following among movie aficionados. Many regard it as Academy Award-winning producer-director Billy Wilder's most successful comedy, as well as Marilyn Monroe's finest performance. Hotel staffers who worked at The Del during the filming recall Monroe as she romped through the hotel halls and played on the beach with Lemmon, Curtis and co-stars George Raft, Joe E. Brown and Pat O'Brien.

The movie is fondly embraced by the management of The Del and the neighboring Coronado and San Diego communities. In fact, a special twenty-fifth anniversary celebration, which honored Lemmon and Curtis and paid special tribute to Wilder, was held in the Grand Ballroom on April 28, 1984. Several hundred citizens, complete with Hollywood celebrities and a host of international media members, attended the gala event which marked the importance of the Hotel del Coronado as a motion picture location site and as a center of social activity.

The last full-length feature film shot at The Del was *The Stunt Man*, starring Peter O'Toole. For those who saw the movie, no, the hotel was not damaged in the least... the famed spiral explodes in the film, but in reality, it was only a model!

By far, the most talked-about celebrity guest in the Hotel del Coronado's almost 100 years of existence was His Royal Highness, the Prince of Wales. He later became King Edward VIII of England, only to abdicate his throne before his coronation for "the woman I love!" The woman he loved was a former Coronado housewife who lived within blocks of The Del. She was the wife of the commanding officer of the nearby North Island Naval Air Station at the time of the prince's visit in April, 1920. (The port of San Diego was a stop on his around-the-world cruise aboard the *HMS Renown.*)

Ever since the royal visit, it has been hotly argued as to whether or not Wallis Warfield Spencer met the prince at the Hotel del Coronado. The occasion was a full fifteen years prior to their "official" introduction in England, when she was married

(Right): Tennis greats of the early 1900s, such as the Sutton sisters (Miss May Sutton depicted), Maurice McLaughlin and Tom Bundy, played on the first lawn tennis courts located across the street from The Del.

(Below): Beginning in 1899, the golf course, as described in the hotel brochure, consisted of "a circular course of nine holes extending over a rolling tract of land. The total distance is 2730 yards. Bunkers and hazards are properly arranged so that the skill of the veteran golfer undergoers a severe test in making the round." By 1900, it had eighteen holes and was 5318 yards in length. Putting greens were 120 feet in diameter, made of asphalt and covered with a thin coat of sand to make them "fast or slow as desired." In 1959, the course was moved to its current site.

(Opposite): Today, the Hotel del Coronado has six lighted championship tennis courts overlooking the blue Pacific. Celebrities and famed professional players frequent these courts.

to a Baltimore businessman and living in London. But there is evidence the two may have at least had a face-to-face exchange of pleasantries at the huge gala in the hotel's Grand Ballroom (in which more than 1000 people jammed to see the world's most eligible bachelor), or the next day aboard the HMS Renown where the prince hosted a tea for the wives of senior U.S. Naval officers. Most likely, Mrs. Spencer met the prince in the receiving line in the Ballroom. (On another evening, a state dinner was hosted for the prince by San Diego Mayor Louis Wilde in the hotel's Crown Room. California Governor W. D. Stevens attended, along with eighty carefully selected guests; there is no evidence Commander Spencer and his wife were invited.) There are unsubstantiated reports that Commander Spencer was out of town—transferred to a new duty assignment. If these reports are true, it is highly unlikely Mrs. Spencer would have attended without an escort. The legend persists that, indeed, the future Duke and Duchess of Windsor met each other for the first time at the Hotel del Coronado—but nobody except the two principals will ever know the details.

Today, there are several reminders of the famous visitor and the mark he left on this grandame of the Pacific. The hotel's gourmet restaurant, the Prince of Wales Restaurant, is named in his honor. The Duke, years later, wrote a letter to the hotel management, complimenting the restaurant's menu and thanking the hotel for the kind remembrance; he experienced few kindnesses after leaving England in 1936. The only known photograph of the prince in the Crown Room was taken during the state dinner. In it, he is seated beside a young woman; the two are deeply engrossed in conversation. The woman was Ellis Spreckels, daughter-in-law of the hotel's owner, John D. Spreckels. A world traveler and a popular socialite in Coronado and San Diego communities, Mrs. Spreckels later was asked the details of her conversation with the prince. "He was mainly interested in Hollywood and the stars," she replied.

In fact, Ellis Spreckels went to London some years later to counsel Mrs. Spencer, her long-time Coronado friend, who was pondering whether or not to marry the British monarch. Mrs. Spreckels' advice is not known, but the world well knows of Mrs. Spencer's final decision.

A hunting party typical of those regularly organized by the Hotel del Coronado in the 1890s. The stained glass window in the upper right hand corner depicts the mythical Indian goddess Califia (for which California was named). This window is now located in the Prince of Wales Restaurant.

Since the 1890s, The Del has been California's premier oceanfront resort.

(Opposite): The picturesque marina on Glorietta Bay across from the Hotel del Coronado.

JEANNE LAWRENCE

The Hotel del Coronado is truly one of the world's most elegant edifices. It is a place where lovers of all ages can come to immerse themselves in one of America's most romantic settings. One of the guiding forces behind the hotel's aura of elegance, romance and historic significance is Jeanne Lawrence, vice chairman of the board. She has made it her goal to recapture the style, grace and sense of grandeur that was the hallmark of Queen Victoria's era in the late nineteenth century.

This petite and stylish lady is comfortable sitting at the corporate conference table beside M. Larry Lawrence, her husband and chairman of the board, directing the huge hotel resort, and she is just as settled in her role as a member of America's top civic and social circles.

"When you visit this grand house, you immediately feel the atmosphere of elegance and expect a level of service such as was found in the great stylish luxury hotels of England and Europe," said Mrs. Lawrence. "We have worked hard to restore many of the old traditions; our annual Victorian Christmas holiday celebration, the grand continental style of dining—a place where couples can enjoy a nostalgic and romantic setting or where families can recapture the sense of togetherness which our fast-paced society often neglects."

Mrs. Lawrence spends hours researching the hotel's vast historical files. She prepares new programs which will recapture many of the old traditions that have been lost over the years. She travels around the world, visiting the remaining luxury hotels and resorts. There she takes careful note of operations and gleans ideas that can be incorporated into the Hotel del Coronado in order to maintain its status as a world-class property. Mrs. Lawrence is currently supervising the hotel's ongoing reservation program. Now a doctoral candidate, she holds a masters degree in business, serves on a number of board nationwide, and chaired the 1988 Centennial Gala Committee which coordinated the yearlong program of the 100th anniversary celebration. "We have a tradition to uphold and my husband and I are striving to maintain and preserve that tradition of elegance, style and grace for generations to come."

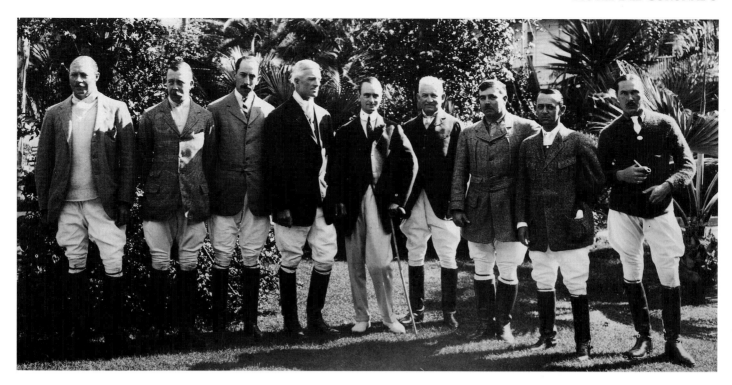

Less ostentatious was the April, 1898, visit by Belgium's heir apparent, Prince Albert. According to newspaper reports, Prince Albert registered at the hotel under an American alias. The San Diego *Union* reporter who uncovered the disguise described the prince as "unpretentious and sensible." These words were meant as a compliment, considering those days of England's Queen Victoria and Europe's royalty.

The Prince of Wales' visit in 1920 created much pomp, ceremony and notoriety. But The Del's first royal visitor was Hawaii's last monarch, King Kalakaua. He came for the Christmas holidays in the 1890s. This popular royal visitor entertained U.S. Army and Naval officers in the parlor adjacent to his suite.

The Del's first recorded social function was in December, 1887, prior to its official opening. The event was a dance held by the management for the staff members who had just come from the East. In those early days, when the hotel first opened, informal dances were a regular occurrence, as were Sunday afternoon band concerts performed by the hotel's own band.

The first meal ever served at the hotel was prepared by Chef M. Frederick Compagnon on December 27, 1887—again, before the official opening—in the Garden Patio. This inaugural meal was enjoyed by the hotel's first manager, J. B. Seghers, his wife, and a party of twenty intimate friends, including owners Elisha Babcock and H. L. Story, and architect James Reid. Today, the Hotel del Coronado has four popular restaurants which serve a wide variety of dishes. These restaurants are favorites with hotel guests and also with the greater San Diego community.

The Hotel del Coronado has been the site of countless social functions over the years. But one of its greatest honors is hosting the annual Charity Ball, one of San Diego's oldest traditions. The Ball began as a benefit for San Diego children in 1909, and is still held at the hotel each year to benefit the Children's Hospital and Health Center. It is regarded as one of San Diego's most prestigious social functions. Other popular social events held at The Del include the Mardi Gras for the Junior of Social Service, the La Jolla Debutante Ball, and the San Diego Chamber of Commerce's annual Flag and General Officer's Ball (which brings together high-ranking military and civilian leaders).

The Del has witnessed San Diego's rich military history, from the days of the Great White Fleet in the 1890s, to Glenn Curtis' first amphibious landing on Coronado, to the mammoth Naval and Marine buildup during World War II. Through the years, as San Diego grew to be one of the nation's foremost military communities, The Del grew to be an important social center for Naval and Marine officers. Eileen Jackson, long-time San Diego *Tribune* social columnist who covered San Diego and Coronado for over forty years, pointed out, "They've always liked the Navy in Coronado. I can recall people saying they enjoy the Navy folks because they are not so provincial; they're well-traveled." Jackson feels the civilian community, like its military neighbors, are also well-traveled and certainly are not provincial.

The British were frequent visitors to the San Diego Naval facilities. The Del served as a favorite entertainment and relaxation haunt because of its English flavor, and also because of its nearby polo facility. This gave our American officers the opportunity to challenge their cousins to polo matches. Eyewitness reports reveal that—somehow—the British didn't get the best horses and oddly enough, our American hosts maintained a certain equestrian advantage during these contests!

Sports of all kinds have attracted visitors to The Del. The huge billiard room used to be the main attraction in the lower portion of the hotel. A bowling alley was also a popular venue, as were yachting and fishing off Coronado's coast.

Today, the Hotel del Coronado is a popular beach and tennis facility. It has one of the most beautiful expanses of sandy beach anywhere in the country and its six lighted tennis courts regularly attract professional players (such as Chris Evert) as well as amateur player-guests.

In the early days, the hotel—and its many recreational amenities—attracted celebrities, heads-of-state, captains of industry, high-ranking military officers and the wealthy. Today, San Diego is California's second largest city and the nation's seventh, and these people can come to the Hotel del Coronado and remain relatively unnoticed. But when the hotel was young and San Diego and Coronado together had less than 20,000 residents, such notables were bound to—and indeed did—make headlines!

In the early 1900s, a group of dashing U.S. Navy officers organized a polo team that elevated Coronado to the polo capital of the world (opposite). The English teams (1910 team depicted above) proved strong opponents.

(Below): Ladies' billiard room, 1888. Billiards reached their peak in popularity during the 1890s. The pastime was soon replaced by automobiles and the moving picture. In 1937, the billiard room and bowling alleys were replaced by the Circus Casino.

PERFECT IN ALL ITS
APPOINTMENTS

As it has been for nearly a century, the white wood and red shingle exterior of the Hotel del Coronado is at once spectacular and strange. Visitors usually see it for the first time from high above San Diego Harbor as they cross the massive span known as the San Diego-Coronado Bay Bridge. The hotel is a grand example of Victorian architecture and is one of the world's best preserved nineteenth century edifices.

Up close, The Del looks as if it emerged not from an architect's grand design, but from a wild fantasy. One can easily understand why this elegant wooden castle by the sea inspired L. Frank Baum to write his famous *Wizard of Oz* series. A draftsman for the Reid Brothers architectural firm commented, upon the hotel's completion, that "it was amazing how many rooms were built that were not even planned at the start of construction."

Everything about the Pacific Coast's largest beach resort—its shapes, lines and even its building materials—is electrifying. Unlike some forms of Victorian architecture, such as the shingle-style, or the stick-style, which are built with a simplicity of material in mind, The Del was constructed with a variety of building material: wood, shingle, glass and brick. The wood selected by the Reid Brothers was of several varieties, none of which is attractive to termites (thus answering one of the frequent questions of hotel guests). Thick planks, some of them up to fifty feet long, make up the framework of the massive Crown and Coronet Rooms, as well as the Grand Ballroom.

On the exterior of the hotel, there are at least four different kinds of cedar shingles along with horizontal shiplap siding and vertical siding, both made of redwood. In addition, there are balconies with lathe-shaped ornamentation. An estimated two million red shingles make up the cover of the hotel's most striking trademark, the one-of-a-kind red roof. Elisha Babcock, the hotel's first owner, felt the red color would link the hotel to San Diego's Spanish mission heritage.

Someone once counted more than 2000 redwood doors in the main building of The Del. This same person also counted 2372 windows. Both window glass and stained glass were used in the original construction, although little of the stained glass has survived the passage of time and the hotel's different renovations.

The hotel will be perfect in all its appointments. The grand front will be immediately on the seaside; the side fronts, both east and west, giving sunshine to every room. Beautifully adorned grounds will adjoin the house, planted with the rarest of tropical flowers. There are spacious verandas, a grand ballroom, rooms en suite and single, with every luxury known to modern ingenuity. Of the cuisine, there shall be nothing to complain, the intent of the managers being to cater to a class of patrons who are accustomed to and who appreciate luxury.

—*Hotel advertising booklet, 1886*

A magnificent view of the tower is evident in this Ocean Towers guest room (above). The Crown Room (above right), has been a popular dining room for guests and local residents for 100 years.

The Hotel del Coronado requires substantial maintenance. A staff of master carpenters, woodwork refinishers and painters work year-round to keep this grand wooden structure in prime condition. For example, it takes a crew of four men ten days just to polish the varnished oak wainscoting (lower panels) which encircle the Crown Room and workers lie on their backs—on scaffolding—in order to apply more than thirty gallons of polish to the ceiling.

At one time, the main building was surrounded by verandas; this was in an era when sitting outdoors in a rocking chair, enjoying the sun and ocean, was a popular pastime. Verandas on the ocean side of The Del have since been enclosed in glass to protect guests from the surf which rolls right to the edge of the building. Originally, the main building had 399 guest rooms and only seventy-five bathrooms. Through the years, verandas and fireplaces were removed in favor of private baths for every room.

Although the Hotel del Coronado is famous for its Victorian architecture, the hotel is actually a combination of several opulent styles associated with the reign of Britain's Queen Victoria. The Del is an outstanding example of the Queen Anne style, distinguished by its uneven design and lack of unity in everything from building materials to cupola design to window shapes.

The wood ornamentation of the exterior and interior is attributed to Charles Locke Eastlake of England, whose book, *Hints on Household Taste*, was popular in the United States during the 1870s and '80s. Though this styling is attributed to him, it was not with his approval. Eastlake was known to be less than enamored of the Western derivation of his work.

As with any great resort, the approach and entrance is crucial. Visitors are greeted with a variety of trees and foliage. One early-day manager planted flowers in the shape of a crown on the lawn. Most photographs or drawings show traffic curling form Orange Avenue toward the ocean and coming to a halt facing Orange Avenue in front of the entrance. The traffic pattern had been altered over the years, but present owner M. Larry Lawrence, changed it to the way it was in 1888. Lawrence has commited himself to restoring this grand structure to its near original state. Today's visitors arrive under a porte cochere which was designed from

This main building guest room, (above), offers a breathtaking view of the Pacific.

The Hotel del Coronado has offered relaxation in luxury, complete with a sweeping view of the Pacific since opening in 1888. Above, (left), an early ocean-view lounge.

original drawings and photographs by former hotel designer Dixon Morrow. It was completed in 1980. The parking attendant's station is a replica of a ticket booth for the old Coronado ferry, which was the only thoroughfare between San Diego and Coronado before the bridge was built in 1969. The palm trees growing on either side of the porte cochere are Mediterranean palms and were transported from Europe.

During the hotel's early years, there were two main entrances on the east side: men would enter through what is now the main lobby entrance while women had a separate entryway about seventy-five feet to the left (toward the ocean). The ladies used this private lobby to relax, freshen up and repair after an arduous journey by train or dusty motorcar. Meanwhile, the men carried on with the usual check-in procedures. Although this practice would appear somewhat discriminatory today, it was actually a luxury for the ladies, who would be spared the activities of the main lobby, such as fishermen displaying their catches of the day.

The hotel's beautifully-appointed foyer serves as a convenient meeting and assembly point. The U.S. Department of the Interior's Historic Landmark plaque is displayed in the main foyer, as are similar proclamations from the San Diego County Board of Supervisors and the Coronado Historical Association.

Flanking the entrance to the Grand Lobby are tall ormolu sconces finished to look like gold, each with nineteen rose-colored lamps or torchiers. These sconces were manufactured in Paris during the gas lamp era and later were wired for electricity and shipped to Montreal before arriving at The Del. The Lobby is one of the Hotel del Coronado's most imposing interior features. The beautifully-polished Illinois oak combined with its unique design makes it one of America's most distinctive hotel lobbies. Other than the furniture, little has changed in the Grand Lobby since 1888. It remains a wonderful example of rich English style and elegance in a most unlikely place—along the California coast near the gates of Mexico!

Beside the sweeping staircase to the mezzanine level, there is the bird-cage electric elevator which has been in operation since the day the hotel opened in 1888.

CENTENNIAL CELEBRATION

T he Hotel del Coronado's yearlong 1988 centennial celebration will come to be known as the grandest spectacle ever witnessed since this Victorian masterpiece opened on February 19, 1888. It would only be fitting that the culmination of a full century as the Pacific Coast's grandame be heralded with unrivaled fanfare and a yearlong program of events, including a Centennial Gala unrivaled in its elegance, performances by some of the nation's top entertainers and exquisite cuisine.

Although a yearlong celebration was planned well in advance of 1988, the crowning point of the anniversary unquestionably would be the Centennial Gala of February 19, 20 and 21. A Centennial committee was formed to ensure that this weekend would be remembered as the grandest in the hotel's history. One of the world's top party coordinators, Wendy Moss of "An Affair to Remember," planned the Centennial Gala weekend. Among other tasks, her crew spent months working on outfitting the hotel for the centennial celebration, ensuring that one of the world's largest dining rooms, the Crown Room, was made to look more elegant than ever before. Lighting crews, seamstresses, fabric companies all teamed to give this National Historic Landmark restaurant, indeed the entire hotel, a new "look" in keeping with tradition but with a fresh eye toward the future.

The weekend began with the hotel's largest and most extraordinary party ever held. Visitors on Friday, February 19, were treated to a station party that encompassed the entire hotel! A 'Some Like It Hot' speakeasy, a Wizard of Oz Emerald City replica, a '50s diner all were recreated through the use of amazing sets and accomplished actors portraying the hotel's most famous guests (Marilyn Monroe, Thomas Edison, Prince of Wales, etc.).

Saturday began with a gorgeous breakfast buffet, followed by a celebrity-filled tennis tournament and a harbor cruise. Gaming tables would be worked round the clock in between time. That evening, the actual Centennial Gala took place in the hotel.

The Food & Beverage Department of the Hotel del Coronado had been waiting for this event for years. Beverly Bass' crew had prepared a magnificent menu for the evening which was presented in the classic style that is the Hotel del Coronado trademark. After this magnificent feast, a star performance greeted the 600 guests in the Grand Ballroom, which had been redecorated by crews who had begun work directly after Friday's opening dinner. After the unforgettable Centennial Gala program, guests retired to the Gaming Room for some midnight fun, and then rested up for Sunday morning's buffet breakfast.

In between scheduled events, guests gazed at the America's Cup, prominently

The centennial celebration program was unveiled to the world on March 19, 1987, when a festive party was held for 500 guests at the hotel. Actors and actresses in historical costumes (top) greeted attendees in the Centennial Pavilion. After owners M. Larry and Jeanne Lawrence (above) recreated the ground-breaking, an elegant luncheon was served in the Crown Room where President and General Manager Scott W. Anderson shared the details of the upcoming centennial and invited guests to enjoy the new history gallery.

displayed in the hotel during the entire weekend.

The Centennial Gala would be an event never to be repeated and never to be forgotten.

But there would still be 10 more months of celebration in store:

One of the physical changes to the hotel for the anniversary year was the addition of a 7,000 square foot Centennial Pavilion, and a new mini-museum called The History Gallery. The Pavilion was constructed next to the tennis courts at beachside, and was built in honor of the famed Coronado Tent City. In the early 1900s it was fashionable to live in tents alongside the hotel, a tradition which lasted 37 years. The pavilion continues to host charity balls and other events.

The History Gallery project was a labor of love for Centennial Committee Chairman Jeanne K. Lawrence; Centennial Coordinator Patricia Anderson; and Linda Evans, who designed this display of historical artifacts and memorabilia. Included are some of the first light bulbs used in the electrical system supervised by Thomas Edison and many hard-to-find photographs of the early, colorful years of the hotel's history.

That historical past would be evident to visitors to the hotel during its 100th anniversary through vignettes performed by actors recreating scenes from the hotel's past on a daily basis. Also every day of the centennial, A Salute to the States food presentation featured regional foods in the hotel's dining rooms.

Along with the return of ferry service to and from San Diego, and a new rubber-wheeled trolley for transporting hotel guests through town, was the restoration of The Oxford. Coronado's oldest public structure was relocated to the hotel and renovated in time for the 1988 centennial. It now houses administrative staff and has resulted in the opening of 12 new meeting rooms in the Grande Hall convention complex thanks to the relocation of staff. Guests in the front of the Ocean Towers building can see this proud structure from their rooms.

Other centennial highlights include a 10K run, various community events, special theme parties for conventions, packages such as the "Del Mar Racetrack" weekend, and a January 1988 reception for media covering the Super Bowl at San Diego's Jack Murphy stadium.

No wonder Kodak picked the Hotel del Coronado as the subject of a 1988 centennial photo essay. And no wonder a Rand McNally publication stated that the Hotel del Coronado "...enjoys more fame and historical significance than perhaps any other hotel in North America." It was true during the hotel's first century and it'll be true for its second.

One of the famous visitors for the 100th anniversary celebration was Snow White, who previewed the February Centennial Gala with a visit to the Centennial Pavilion (top left). Children dressed as newsboys handed out leaflets on the centennial program during the March 19 Centennial Preview party (top right).

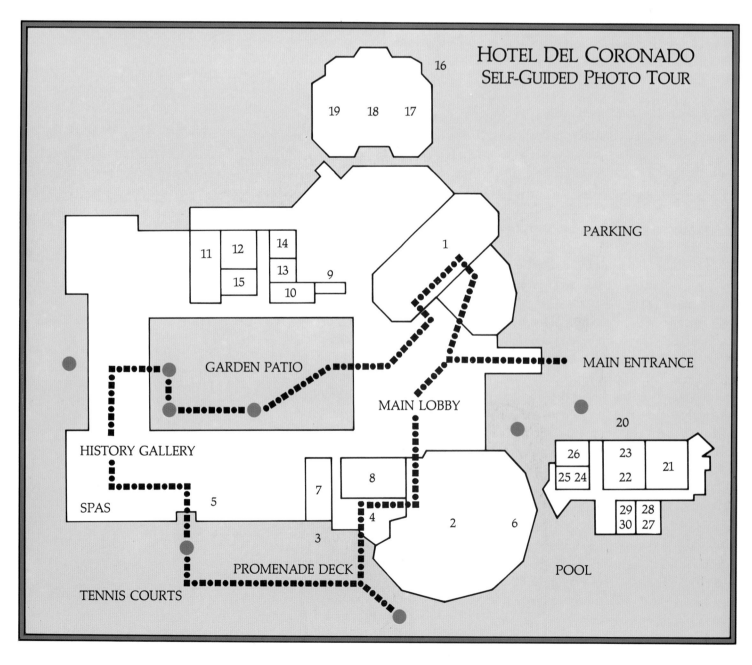

HOTEL DEL CORONADO
SELF-GUIDED PHOTO TOUR

16

19   18   17

PARKING

11   12   14

13

15   10

9

1

GARDEN PATIO

MAIN ENTRANCE

MAIN LOBBY

20

HISTORY GALLERY

26   23

25 24   22   21

SPAS   5

7

8

4

29 28

30 27

3

PROMENADE DECK

2   6

POOL

TENNIS COURTS

(Opposite): The Hotel del Coronado's lobby has changed very little since opening in 1888 as these two photos, taken nearly 100 years apart, illustrate.

The Del's newest addition, Palm Court, left, faces on the Garden Patio and recalls the hotel's sun porches of an earlier era.

In the early years, the mezzanine was known as "the gallery," a place where ladies could sit, visit or watch the lobby traffic below. "The gallery is much frequented by the ladies," proclaims a piece of early advertisment. "Thither they resort for friendly social converse and to see newcomers entering below and registering their names."

If there is a queen of rooms it would be the Crown Room. Here, under the sugar pine ceiling which rises thirty-three feet, is one of the largest pillar-free rooms in North America. Huge state dinners for presidents, princes and heroes have been held in this room which measures 156 feet by sixty-six feet. Charles Lindbergh was feted here a few months after his historic solo flight across the Atlantic in 1927; Britain's Prince of Wales (later King Edward VIII, then Duke of Windsor) was hosted to a grand dinner in 1920; and more than 1000 guests—the largest state dinner ever held in San Diego County—were invited by President Richard Nixon as he honored Mexican President Gustavo Diaz Ordaz.

Originally, the Crown Room was the hotel's only dining room. But other facilities have since come into play and today the Crown Room is used for elegant evening dining and occasionally for breakfast and lunch when the adjacent Coronet Room cannot accommodate the demand. The Crown Room is also used for a number of special functions throughout the year: it is the scene of holiday dining on Easter, Mother's Day, Thanksgiving, Christmas and New Year's and plays host to the annual Sweetheart Dinner-Dance on Valentine's Day. The Crown Room's weekly Sunday brunch, which is served from 9 a.m. to 2 p.m., is probably the most popular dining spot in all of San Diego County. A lavish display of food is placed on long tables, providing an unequaled selection of delicacies. What makes the Crown Room so spectacular is its size, and knowing that the room was constructed without visible posts or pillars, and that the beautiful high-paneled ceiling was placed without nails but rather with wooden pegs. In a word, the Crown Room is breathtaking!

The Coronet Room, the smaller dining room adjacent to the Crown Room, measures fifty-eight feet by sixty-six feet and has a ceiling height of twenty-seven feet. Despite its intimate size (small when compared to its bigger brother), the Coronet Room has had its days of glory. Here, on October 8, 1982, President

HOTEL DEL CORONADO
SELF-GUIDED PHOTO TOUR

1 CROWN/CORONET ROOM
2 GRAND BALLROOM
3 OCEAN TERRACE
4 OCEAN TERRACE LOUNGE
5 PRINCE OF WALES RESTAURANT
6 INTERNATIONAL ROOM
7 WINDSOR ROOM
8 CRYSTAL/CONTINENTAL ROOM
9 EXECUTIVE ROOM
10 GARDEN ROOM
11 HANOVER ROOM
12 STUART ROOM
13 YORK ROOM
14 KENT ROOM
15 TUDOR ROOM
16 GRANDE HALL
17 OXFORD HALL
18 REGENT HALL
19 EMPRESS HALL
20 POOLSIDE
21 DOVER ROOM
22 STRATFORD ROOM
23 DURHAM ROOM
24 SOMERSET ROOM
25 BRADFORD ROOM
26 MANCHESTER ROOM
27 CARDIF ROOM
28 LANCASTER ROOM
29 PEMBROOK ROOM
30 LEEDS ROOM

(Above): Guests from around the world flock to the hotel for its traditional holiday celebration. The Victorian Christmas tree, which stands thirty feet tall in the lobby, is the grand attraction during the hotel's annual holiday celebration. December boasts a month-long calendar of events including chorale performances, holiday teas and, of course, the tree lighting ceremony held the first week of the month.

(Opposite): The popular Prince of Wales Restaurant specializes in exotic after-dinner coffees such as the flaming "Cafe Diable" as prepared by Maitre D' Stephen Schakne.

(Preceding Pages): The Crown Room is the Del's original dining room and is opened for elegant evening meals.

(Below): Regal crest adorns the Prince of Wales Restaurant, the Hotel del Coronado's world famous gourmet restaurant.

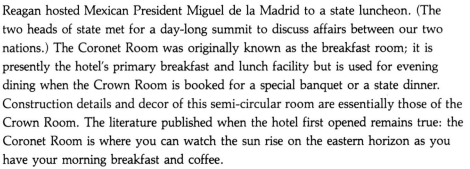

Reagan hosted Mexican President Miguel de la Madrid to a state luncheon. (The two heads of state met for a day-long summit to discuss affairs between our two nations.) The Coronet Room was originally known as the breakfast room; it is presently the hotel's primary breakfast and lunch facility but is used for evening dining when the Crown Room is booked for a special banquet or a state dinner. Construction details and decor of this semi-circular room are essentially those of the Crown Room. The literature published when the hotel first opened remains true: the Coronet Room is where you can watch the sun rise on the eastern horizon as you have your morning breakfast and coffee.

If the Hotel del Coronado has another star among its great public rooms it is the Grand Ballroom located under the great tower on the south end of the main lobby. This magnificent room has served as a theater and a concert hall; it has also been the site of a number of gala balls over the years. In 1920, the Royal Ball for the Prince of Wales was held in this room and the San Diego community hosted a large reception (with more than 1000 guests) for President Jimmy Carter in 1979.

In the early years, the Grand Ballroom had a high ceiling and included a balcony. Guests could stroll around the balcony and look out the upper windows at the ocean below. This was altered in 1960. Today, the Grand Ballroom serves as a theatrical and entertainment facility for conventions and as a ballroom for college fraternities and charity organization. San Diegans love to transform the Grand Ballroom into a spectacular showplace with flowers, big band music and elegantly decorated tables.

There are those who believe the Hotel del Coronado was built merely to surround one of Southern California's most beautiful courtyards—and, they may be right! The Garden Patio is a popular retreat: guests can sit and enjoy the warm sun, couples can exchange wedding vows, corporations can treat shareholders and clients to an elegant lawn reception. Interestingly enough, none of the many subtropical plants are indigenous to San Diego—all were introduced from abroad! Included among the beautiful flora are Mexican Guadalupe palms, a Brazilian Blue Jelly palm and Kentia palms from Australia's Lord Howe Island. There is a lonely male Cycad (a remnant of the prehistoric age),

(Above): Outdoor dining at The Del.

(Below): Hotel del Coronado History Gallery.

(Opposite, above): Sunset at The Del.

(Opposite, below): Hotel entrance from the South.

a tall King palm with its skirt of seeds blowing in the wind, and a tall well-groomed Lady palm from China. The Garden Patio also has fuchsias, birds of paradise and philodendrons.

The main attraction of the central courtyard is a wonderfully crafted gazebo, engineered by hotel designer Dixon Morrow and constructed by staff carpenters. Morrow, who has been instrumental in restoring the hotel to its original state, discovered an early photograph of the Garden Patio which included a gazebo. Morrow went to work and designed the structure to match, almost identically, the one that had long since been torn down and forgotten. "Mr. (Larry) Lawrence is committed to restoring and keeping this old girl in as near original condition as possible and when I told him about the forgotten gazebo, he directed me to proceed with the construction of a new one," said Morrow. Today, unsuspecting visitors would never have guessed that the courtyard's gazebo is less than ten years old. This is a tribute to the hotel craftsmen and to their ability to replicate woodwork which equals that of the nineteenth century masters.

The hotel has accommodated history buffs by designating an entire lower passage as "The History Gallery." It is located at the west end of the Garden Patio and down one flight of stairs. This intriguing walk takes visitors back 100 years with displays of hotel office and telephone equipment, cooking utensils, tools used in construction, original electric lamps that Thomas Edison helped install, an example of an early guest room and photos and architectural drawings of the hotel's construction. A large display of earlier photographs is located in the lower lobby on the east side of the hotel, beside the Del Deli.

The Deli is a most interesting place to eat; it has literally been carved out of what was once the hotel's rainwater storage cistern. (Not only did these huge concrete tanks supply the needs of the hotel but in the early days, they supplied the entire city of Coronado as well.) Doors connecting the various maze-like cistern rooms were cut with jackhammers through four-foot-thick concrete walls. Guests can easily see what an enormous task it was to create, but what a delightful place it is today! The Deli is open around-the-clock and serves sandwiches, salads, soups, beer and wine, and pastries.

Within full view of the ocean, visitors can sit and enjoy breakfast, lunch or their favorite cocktail in The Del's Ocean Terrace Room and Bar. This sidewalk/indoor cafe and bar is magically transformed into a cabaret with live entertainment for evening dancing and listening pleasure. The Ocean Terrrace Room and Bar is paneled in rich Philippine mahogany and is accented in a bright green wool. The magnificent wooden bar was build in 1895 by the Brunswick Company of Pennsylvania; it was shipped around Cape Horn to California. This grand example of handcrafted woodwork is held together with pegs and dowels. The bar has an ornate gazebo with a statue of a blackamoor in the center and a cappuccino machine behind the bar. The ceiling is original.

The newest addition to The Del's dining facilities is the Prince of Wales Restaurant, located at the end of the hall (down from the Ocean Terrace Bar). Opened in 1970, this luxuriously intimate dining room is richly-appointed in mahogany—in the English tradition—with a magnificent British Royal insignia draped by Old Glory and the Union Jack over the fireplace. The Prince of Wales Restaurant is noted throughout Southern California for its gourmet fare, and its wine list is one of the largest on this side of the Mississippi River.

Directly below the Grand Ballroom, off the Ocean Terrace Bar, is the International Room. At one time it was the stage for the famed performer, Liberace; the popular pianist performed here during the summers of 1949 and 1950 when it was known as the Circus Room. Other performers to appear in the old Circus Room were the "incomparable" Hildegard and the Ames Brothers. Today, the International Room serves as a ballroom, a meeting room or a banquet facility.

Back in the main lobby area, in what used to be the ladies billiard room, is the Lobby Shop, where newspapers, magazines, gifts, souvenirs, liquor, toiletries and sundry items can be found.

YESTERDAY'S

GRAND HOTEL TODAY AND TOMORROW

It is doubtful that anyone would plan an elegant Victorian structure in today's world, especially in Southern California where brass, glass and rustic wood are primary decor items. The Hotel del Coronado, to all outward appearances, belongs to a time when there were no automobiles, radios or televisions. The Del was born into an era when the telephone was a remote luxury and the incandescent light bulb was a new-fangled invention that probably wouldn't last. (There's proof of this in the hotel's History Gallery where an original electric light fixture is on display, complete with natural gas lamps which were built on each side of the bulb—just in case the electricity or the bulb failed!)

Edmund Wilson wrote in his 1931 book, "You feel that you can still enjoy here (at the Hotel del Coronado) the last moment before the power of American money...had finally turned its back altogether on the human tastes and habits of the old non-mechanical world."

But appearances are deceiving: the Hotel del Coronado has not only remained alive, it is constantly riding the crest of technology by offering the latest in hotel, restaurant and convention facilities. All of this has happened over the years because the private ownership, which has changed hands only five times in 100 years, has insisted that the hotel adapt itself to the demands of a changing world.

Back in 1888, when the hotel first opened, the latest technological innovation was the electric light. Thomas Edison himself traveled West to supervise the installation of his system into the hotel. The three Otis elevators, still in operation today, carry the serial numbers 061, 062 and 063; Otis has since built more than 2.5 million elevators. Another innovation of 1880s technology was an electric guest call and fire alarm system called an "annunciator." The installations of the annunciator and electric light systems were among the largest in the nation. The annunciator used 350 battery cells and 1900 pounds of copper wire. The incandescent light power plant, one of the first built in the state of California, boasted five Mather-type dynamos, two with a capacity to light 400 lights each and the other three capable of lighting 250 each. The Del's installation of electrical lighting, the largest west of New York City, made major headlines in 1888. One newspaper account

(Above): The Hotel del Coronado's famed Dracaena Draco ("Dragon tree") was planted shortly after the hotel was built in 1887, and is one of the very few growing in North America. This rare liliaceous tree originates in China and the Canary Islands.

(Opposite): One of Southern California's most spectacular views can be found on the Promenade Deck overlooking the ocean—a popular spot for catered parties. It overlooks the hotel's Olympic-sized pool, one of two pools at the hotel. The other is located by the Ocean Towers building.

(Following pages): The Hotel del Coronado and its beachside swimming and tennis facilities, as a storm breaks at dusk.

reported, "The mammoth building, illuminated with its hundreds of electric lights, presented a picture that will not easily be effaced from the memories of those who were present." Another newspaper story covered a fancy dress social ball, reporting that guests took time out from dancing in the Grand Ballroom to go down to the basement, through the tunnel, to the electric plant and inspect this modern-day marvel. As fascinating as the electric light was, there were still those guests who were dubious of its advantages. Each guest room had a small card prominently displayed, stating, "This room is equipped with the Edison Electric Light. Do not attempt to light with a match. Simply turn key on the wall by the door. The use of electricity for lighting is in no way harmful to health, nor does it affect soundness of sleep." (One of these original cards is on display in the hotel's Hall of History, alongside one of the early light fixtures.)

Today, the power plant is still directly across from the main entrance of the hotel. It is readily identifiable by the large smokestack which has been carefully preserved and is considered an important part of this National Historic Landmark.

The Hotel del Coronado is also cognizant of the world's need for energy conservation. To this end, the hotel maintains efficient energy production through its co-generation plant and solar power collection system. The Del has sixteen large solar collectors on the roof of the Grande Hall which produce one percent of the hotel's electrical needs and five percent of its hot water. The hotel's solar photovoltaic system ensures that the backup batteries for the house computer are kept charged at all times. Additional hot water is produced by a heat harvesting system which captures waste heat from the air-conditioning system in the Ocean Towers complex, thus reducing natural gas consumption by about twenty-five percent. About one-third of the hotel's electricity is produced by an 800-kilowatt natural gas-fired turbine generator system below the Grande Hall. This co-generation system also supplies high pressure steam for the hotel's laundry facilities, the two spas, and the kitchens; the guest room heating, which is also supplied by this system, is recovered from hot exhaust gases.

SCOTT W. ANDERSON

Scott W. Anderson is far better prepared for his role as general manager of The Del than was Elisha Babcock (who found himself in charge six months after the hotel was built.) Babcock's best qualification for this lofty position was his sense of humor; Anderson, after years of hotel grooming, is far better qualified! The myriad details of running this sprawling resort, with its nearly 1,200 hotel workers, are overseen by Anderson (who is also president of the Hotel del Coronado Corporation), and by eleven senior vice-presidents, and thirty-seven managers, department heads and supervisors.

A native of San Diego, Anderson was groomed for hotel management in grand fashion, receiving a degree in hotel and restaurant administration from Washington State University after which he worked seven years for Westin Hotels in Los Angeles, Orange County and Phoenix. He joined the Hotel del Coronado as vice president and resident manager in 1979, but it was not his first time at The Del. Anderson began working at the famed beach resort as a high school teenager; he was a swimming pool attendant and lifeguard before working in a number of jobs including bellman, desk clerk, kitchen aide, cook, parking attendant, housekeeper and laundry helper. (He helped prepare more than 1,000 salads for the huge Nixon-Ordaz State Dinner in The Crown Room in 1971).

Anderson was elected president of the San Diego Hotel-Motel Association in 1984, and is active in a number of other civic and professional organizations, including the San Diego Children's Hospital where he is a trustee, the Coronado Chamber of Commerce (director), San Diego Convention & Visitors Bureau (director), San Diego Community Colleges Advisory Board and Coronado Hotel-Motel Association of which he is chairman.

One of Anderson's proudest moments was being a part of a joint civic committee responsible for bringing the National Football League's annual Super Bowl to San Diego in 1988, Centennial anniversary year of the Hotel del Coronado.

Anderson was named San Diego's "Outstanding Young Citizen" in 1982, and was runner-up for this prestigious annual Jaycee award in 1984.

Photo taken the morning of Opening Day, February 19, 1888 on the hotel's back porch. Of the two men with knives in their belts, the one on the left was the famous Chef de Cuisine Frederick Pierre Compagnon.

A CITY WITHIN A CITY

The Del's kitchens alone have staffs that could keep a number of small towns in America well fed. The staff is a good indication of just how many meals are served in any one twenty-four-hour period: there are two executive chefs, four sous chefs, seventy-six cooks, eight bakers, a butcher, a pastry chef, a wine steward, six hosts and hostesses, eleven captains, 113 servers, seventy-five busboys, eighteen bartenders, nine barboys and thirteen cocktail servers.

An average of 2500 meals a day come out of the central kitchen (large enough to contain two basketball courts). On special holidays, such as Thanksgiving and Christmas, that figure can rise to 6000 or more! The refrigerated food storage area in the lower level of the hotel covers nearly an acre. Breakfasts and lunches for the Ocean Terrace indoor and outdoor cafes are provided by the Prince of Wales Restaurant kitchen, because the gourmet restaurant is only open during dinner hours (6 p.m. to 10:30 p.m.)

Hotel owner M. Larry Lawrence and Vice Chairman of the Board Jeanne Lawrence share a moment with the Hotel del Coronado kitchen staff.

The hotel's security staff contains veteran police officers who, collectively, have more than 200 years of experience with local, state and federal agencies. The Coronado Police Department, which has a smaller number of officers, often calls upon the hotel's security department to assist them in such areas as language translation (more than twenty-four foreign languages are spoken by the huge staff).

The Del's maintenance department is one of the largest of any hotel in the world. There are twenty painters on the maintenance payroll alone; in addition, there are ten carpenters and assistants, assorted electricians and plumbers.

The hotel's laundry facility is one of the largest in San Diego County. Not only does it handle the bedding and dining room linens for the hotel, but it also handles laundry needs for more than twenty other hotels and motels in the area.

Because of the unique decoration demands of the hotel (no two rooms of the main building are alike in size, shape or decoration), there is an upholstery shop. Its sole purpose is to recondition the hotel's furniture.

The carpentry shop provides handmade items to replace, match or add to those which cannot be obtained elsewhere.

A DIRECTORY OF THE HOTEL DEL CORONADO'S SERVICES

Among the many treasures of the Hotel del Coronado are a wide array of services and retail specialties for our guests. You will find their descriptions in the following pages.

CREATE MEMORIES AND A TRADITION

ACCENT GIFTS, located in the Lower Lobby Shopping Arcade, offers unique silver handmade gifts. Browse through ACCENT GIFTS and add to your memorable experience at the legendary Hotel del Coronado with custom-made designs. We ship anywhere in the world. Special gifts are elegant as well as affordable at ACCENT GIFTS!

FOR THE FASHIONABLE MAN

BRADY'S offers a complete line of clothing for men: sport coats, Ultra-suede, suits, sport shirts, sweaters, slacks, and swimwear. Such names as Halston, LeBaron, St. Croix, Nautica, Boathouse Row, Gant, to mention a few, are blended with an extensive selection of BRADY'S own collection. This complete line of men's fashions is bound to enhance your wardrobe. Located in the Lower Lobby Shopping Arcade, BRADY'S is open seven days a week, 9 a.m. to 10 p.m. We welcome Visa, Mastercard, American Express, Diners Club and Carte Blanche charge cards.

WHAT'S IN A NAME?

Regardless of your nationality, it is quite likely that your name has been registered at some point in history as the bearer of a crest or coat of arms. You are invited to peruse the 250,000 names on record in the delightful BRITISH IMPORTING COMPANY. The staff is well-informed and there is no charge for information. Family crests are available and are priced from $9.95 to $895. The BRITISH IMPORTING COMPANY is located in the Lower Lobby Shopping Arcade of the Hotel del Coronado.

A WORLD OF TOYS

Travel down the Yellow Brick Road of the Lower Lobby Shopping Arcade to CHILDREN'S WORLD. One of the most unique toy shops along the Pacific coast, we have educational toys and a large variety of souvenir T-shirts from around the world for children of all ages. Take a special toy home to a special child to remind him of your memorable visit to the Hotel del Coronado.

IT'S CHRISTMAS YEAR-ROUND

"Live the spirit of Christmas every day" at CHRISTMAS 1888, the shop that specializes in nativities, pyramids, Christmas china, dated collectibles and unusual ornaments from around the world. The owners of CHRISTMAS 1888 travel to Europe, where Christmas decorations originated, to find the unusual and traditional. The store's 16 decorated trees depict different themes and seasons, from Easter to Valentine's Day. CHRISTMAS 1888, located in the Lower Level Shopping Arcade near the Hotel del Coronado's front outside entrance, is open daily until 10:30 p.m.

A GALLERY OF CLASSICS

The lobby of the Hotel del Coronado features San Diego County's largest, most diversified collection of fine art graphics with posters and reproductions by famous artists. You can make your visit even more memorable by taking home a treasure from CORONADO GALLERY—fine art at realistic prices —completely framed and ready to hang. Don't worry about transporting your new purchase: we ship anywhere in the Continental United States!

A LEGEND IN FASHION

A legend within a legend, COURY'S RESORT APPAREL has been a tradition with Hotel del Coronado guests and visitors since 1953. Known as "the Boutique of the Pacific," COURY's offers personal service and selective apparel unlike any boutique of its size. At COURY's you'll find the latest in dresses, sportswear, local designs, swimwear, casual wear, and a fascinating line of accessories. Don't worry if you have forgotten to pack those necessary items: we have everything you need for the "beach to the ballroom." COURY's is located in the Lower Lobby Shopping Arcade, directly in front of the elevator and stairs which lead to the Grand Lobby.

FLOWERS FIT FOR A CROWN

No matter what the occasion, whether it's celebrating your wedding anniversary at the Hotel del Coronado or just saying, "I'm thinking of you," the DEL CORONADO FLORISTS will meet your every floral need in a variety of arrangements made with the finest and freshest of beautiful flowers. Located in the Lower Lobby Shopping Arcade, the DEL CORONADO FLORISTS also offer a large assortment of silk flowers and many beautiful gifts. In addition, we do arrangements for private parties, conventions and weddings.

A GEM WITHIN A GEM

DEL CORONADO JEWELS, located in the Lower Lobby Shopping Arcade of the Hotel del Coronado, specializes in fun and fashion jewelry. Established in 1952, DEL CORONADO JEWELS is the exclusive representative of Panetta, the finest name in costume jewelry. We have an extensive selection of Crown Jewelry for that special remembrance of your stay at the hotel. We also offer a large selection of fourteen-carat charms and fine jewelry. You'll find the finest quality Cubic Zirconia in custom mountings, with many one-of-a-kind stones, some of which are imported from Switzerland and set by our own craftsmen. Complimentry ring and jewelry cleaning for Hotel guests is available at DEL CORONADO JEWELS.

THE WORLD IS OUR BUSINESS

The DEL CORONADO TRAVEL AGENCY is conveniently located in the History Gallery, across from the beauty salon. Agency experts, offering the finest possible travel services, specialize in arranging post-meeting trips and tours to any point on the globe. Equipped with the latest in computerized technology, the DEL CORONADO TRAVEL AGENCY's professional staff provides personal consultation and attention to detail. For your next trip to the fabulous Hotel del Coronado, call the DEL CORONADO TRAVEL AGENCY at: (619) 522-8144.

ROUND THE CLOCK DELI DELIGHTS

The Hotel del Coronado's classic DEL DELI will please every palate. Located in the Lower Lobby, the DEL DELI has been carved out of the huge fresh water cistern which provided the hotel's water supply during the early days. With its four-foot-thick walls, the DEL DELI is filled with marvelous sandwiches, salads, fresh fruits, soft drinks, fresh pastries from the hotel's bakery, and both foreign and domestic beers and wines. Open 24 hours a day.

RENT A CAR, AND A COMPANY

Enjoy the scenic wonder of San Diego County at your leisure with the freedom of an affordable DOLLAR RENT A CAR. You are always guaranteed high quality and personalized service. Choose from a wide selection of clean, comfortable late model cars. We are conveniently located on the grounds of the elegant Hotel del Coronado and are open to serve you seven days a week, 8:00 a.m. to 5:00 p.m. Group arrangements also available. (619) 435-6611, ext. 7194 (619) 437-1739

IMPORTED ACCESSORIES FOR THAT SPECIAL PERSON

FASHION ACCENT offers the finest and most exclusive selection of ladies' handbags and travel accessories for men and women. Personal leather goods, luggage and a wide variety of gifts are offered. Located in the Lower Lobby Shopping Arcade of the Hotel del Coronado, FASHION ACCENT has many one-of-a-kind handbags. All major credit cards are accepted; we are open seven days a week.

FOR SPECIAL OR UNEXPECTED OCCASIONS

The HOTEL DEL CORONADO BEAUTY SALON is at your service seven days a week, offering full services for both men and women. Our trained and experienced staff also offers manicures, pedicures, facials and body waxing. Located in the History Gallery next to the spa, we also offer a complete line of Aida Grey cosmetics along with lessons in makeup application. Walk-ins are welcome; we offer the latest in styles of quick comb-outs for those unexpected dinner engagements. Open 9 a.m. daily; evenings by appointment; Sundays noon to 6 p.m. Parking is validated. Dial 7328 from your hotel room phone.

TREAT YOUR BODY TO A ROYAL SPA

The HOTEL DEL CORONADO SPA facilities are among the best in Southern California; they come complete with exercise rooms, steam rooms, saunas and large whirlpool baths. The spa offers separate facilities for men and women; the finest in massages is available. Treat your body to a great experience today, while visiting the world-renowned Hotel del Coronado. The spa is open at 10 a.m. daily.

THE LUXURY OF CASHMERE

Stop by the HOUSE OF CASHMERE in the Lower Lobby Shopping Arcade of the Hotel del Coronado and enjoy the luxury of romantic cashmere clothing. Over fifty different styles of sweaters, dresses and vests including cardigans, V-necks, crew necks and turtlenecks are available in solids, argyles, intarsias and embroideries. These items are affordably priced, with up to seventy percent off what you would normally pay for these fine imported articles of clothing. We accept phone orders, because it is easy for our experienced staff to assist you by describing styles and colors. For phone orders call (800) 325-0276 or (800) 826-7150.

CREATE YOUR OWN FRAGRANCE

HOUSE OF VERSAILLES, located in the Lower Lobby of the world-renowned Hotel del Coronadoo, is simply irresistible for the woman wishing to experience that special magic and be *sans faute!* Fragrance is beauty and beauty is the stimulant to passion. With aroma, all things are possible. The past recaptured and the future changed! Create a memory or live a legend. Be lavish in its use and wear your personal fragrance where you want to be touched. Perhaps a rare and beautiful moment may last a lifetime. Custom blending by appointment; pH and fragrance compatibility analysis available and a selection of imported crystal perfume bottles and atomizers. See the world famous Lomas collection of perfume bottles that once belonged to the famous and infamous.

GENERATIONS OF INTEGRITY IN GEMS

Joe Jessop left his native England in 1890, and headed for America when the Hotel de Coronado was only two years old. Today, GEORGE CARTER JESSOP JEWELERS and the Hotel del Coronado are both legendary names, known for quality service for nearly 100 years. George Carter Jessop continues the family tradition in the Grand Lobby of the Hotel del Coronado. GEORGE CARTER JESSOP JEWELERS offers the finest in gems, watches and jewelry. For exquisite gifts, visit George, who is a certified gemologist of the American Gem Society and is a senior member of the American Society of Appraisers.

FOR YOUR PERSONAL & GIFT NEEDS

The LOBBY SHOP, located next to the Grand Lobby, is your convenience store for personal toiletries, tobacco, liquor, snacks, newspapers, magazines, the latest books and an assortment of giftware. You may wish to borrow a Polaroid camera with your purchase of film or rent a self-guided audio tour for a stroll-through history. For that special memento of your stay at the Hotel del Coronado, we invite you to browse among a variety of items in the Lobby Shop that reflect the Hotel del Coronado heritage. Open daily, 6:00 a.m. to midnight.

CAPTURE THE DEL ON CANVAS

Nationally-known Coronado artist Sue Tushingham McNary has her own art gallery at the Hotel del Coronado which features etchings, oils, acrylics, limited edition collector plates and miniatures of the hotel as well as San Diego, floral, boat and landscape scenes. Sue Tushingham McNary's work reflects a special merger of mature artistic talent and carefully-honed technical skill. Each etching and oil uniquely transforms her sensitive and perceptive interpretation of the world into a permanent visual record of enduring beauty and worth. McNARY'S ART GALLERY is located in the Lower Lobby Shopping Arcade of the hotel. The phone number is (619) 435-1819.

A UNIQUE GIFT GALLERY

THE MOLE HOLE specializes in items from around the world and is the place to go to pick up that special gift. Original works, many by local artists, can be purchased here; nearly one-third of the creations are specially made for THE MOLE HOLE. One-of-a-kind, unique and dramatic interior decorator pieces are displayed in a casual elegant atmosphere. For that unexpected pleasure and treat, stop by THE MOLE HOLE.

OUTDOOR DINING BY THE SEA

The most spectacular dining experience on the North American Pacific Coast is yours when you breakfast or lunch on the scenic OCEAN TERRACE of the world-famous Hotel del Coronado. The sounds of the surf, the scent of the sea and the gentle gliding of the gulls are the tapestry setting for this delightfully romantic restaurant at one of the world's truly great seaside resorts. In the evening, the OCEAN TERRACE LOUNGE provides live music for your listening and dancing pleasure as you enjoy a cocktail with that special person. It's all here for you to savor in the historic atmosphere of the Hotel del Coronado.

DISTINCTIVE DINING

The "distinctive dining experience" of the famed PRINCE OF WALES RESTAURANT in the Hotel del Coronado is more than a phrase; it is the perfect description of the service and cuisine of this popular gourmet restaurant. Impeccable in every detail, the gourmet cuisine of the PRINCE OF WALES RESTAURANT turns dining into the special occasion that matches your special visit to the legendary Hotel del Coronado. For a memorable, delightful evening, plan an elegant dinner in the PRINCE OF WALES RESTAURANT, open daily from 6 p.m. to 10:30 p.m. Reservations are suggested. Dial 7235 from your hotel room phone.

LET US TAKE YOU THERE

Your visit to the Hotel del Coronado can be made even more enjoyable through use of one of the many services of SAN DIEGO EXPRESS. We provide transportation to and from the airport. SAN DIEGO EXPRESS gives tours to the San Diego Zoo, Wild Animal Park, Sea World, San Diego metropolitan area, Harbor Excursions, and Tijuana, Mexico. Visitors can charter a mini-bus or limousine. Conveniently located in Coronado, call us at (619) 435-6611 ext. 7189 or (619) 437-4870.

AN OCEAN OF SHELLS

SHELL WORLD, located in the Lower Lobby Shopping Arcade of the Hotel del Coronado, is filled with unique artistic creations made from natural seashells. Home of the finest custom-designed shell and coral jewelry, SHELL WORLD features specimen shells, and individually-made seashell floral arrangements and shell candles. We also offer a fine selection of nautical gifts and home furnishings to complement a variety of decorative schemes. For the perfect gift for that special occasion, come to SHELL WORLD. Dial 7337 from your hotel room phone, or call (619) 437-1424 when outside the hotel. We're locally owned and operated!

WORLD CLASS FURS

SYDNEY'S FURS is a unique gift and apparel store with one-of-a-kind items from around the world! It features a wide variety of gifts from mink Teddy Bears and baby booties to Chinese shearling mosaic rugs. Visit us for a selection of fine apparel from fox flings to mink coats. SYDNEY'S FURS is located in the Lower Lobby Shopping Arcade in the Hotel del Coronado.

TENNIS, ANYONE?

The Hotel del Coronado is considered one of the great tennis resorts of the world. Don't miss our courtside TENNIS SHOP which offers a variety of casual and signature apparel for both men and women. For your convenience, racquet rentals are available as well as tennis instruction and court reservations.

A SPECIAL CORNER

VICTORIAN CORNER, located in the Lower Lobby Shopping Arcade of the Hotel del Coronado, offers gifts of elegance. An unusual spectrum of collectibles and antiques is available, including hand-cut crystal, French Limoges, Llardo, Royal Doulton, Hummel, Delft, Beatrix Potter, clowns and music boxes. This spectacular selection is bound to appeal to the most discriminating shopper.

SWEET MEMORIES

WINDSOR CHOCOLATES, located in the Lower Lobby Shopping Arcade of the Hotel del Coronado, is the most tasteful and original way to say you care, no matter what the moment might be. The finest in handmade chocolates are available, including dipped strawberries and imported candies. Stop by and watch us make our mouth-watering fudge, dipped fruits and chocolates.

The Hotel del Coronado has been known as a family resort since its opening in 1888. Some of the early recreational activities for children were pony-drawn carts as shown above, circa 1895.

A LIVING LEGEND

A CELEBRATION OF THE DEL

BEACH FRONT RESORT The Hotel del Coronado is the largest full-service beachfront resort on the North American Pacific Coast. From Anchorage to Acapulco, there is no other facility that equals the grandeur, the elegance or the service provided by The Del. Guests can enjoy the Pacific surf outside their guest rooms or suite windows. But most guests don't just come to look out their windows; they come to walk and to play on the wonderful white sandy beach, to play tennis on one of the six lighted clay courts, to swim in the Olympic-size swimming pool, to surf, to fish or to rent a sailboat at nearby Glorietta Bay, or to golf on the finely manicured fairways and greens of the Coronado Golf Course, which is just a few short blocks (within walking distance) from the hotel.

TENNIS The Del is regularly included on lists of the world's finest tennis resorts. Frequently top professional stars, such as Chris Evert, stop by for a relaxing weekend of beach and sun and, of course, to play a couple sets of tennis with Ben Press, the popular hotel pro. (The City of Coronado provides an additional fourteen tennis courts to supplement those at The Del. Tennis buffs will find the game a bit different here. The nearby ocean puts moisture on the ball, making the game a little slower, but more of a challenge!)

GOLF As mentioned, the Coronado Golf Course is located conveniently nearby, but there are a number of other fine courses throughout San Diego County. Torrey Pines, north of La Jolla, is the site of the annual Andy Williams San Diego Open. This is just one of more than fifty courses in the greater San Diego area.

BOATING Sailboating is a popular nautical sport. But if this isn't quite your cup of tea, a cruise around San Diego Bay in a harbor excursion boat is a calmer alternative. Or you can opt for one of the whale-watching boats, which go out to the open sea and travel alongside migrating grey whales.

SAN DIEGO Landlubbers enjoy San Diego for its world famous San Diego Zoo. But the city also offers the Wild Animal Park, Sea World and cultural attractions such as the Old Globe Theater located in beautiful Balboa Park. Besides the Old Globe, Balboa Park offers a number of fine museums, including the Aerospace Museum (which displays a collection of vintage aircraft) and the Reuben E. Fleet Space Theater. San Diego also has a fine opera company, and symphony and pop orchestras that give regularly scheduled performances throughout the year. There are also more than thirty community playhouses in San Diego County, including the Coronado Playhouse, which is less than four blocks from the hotel!

TIJUANA The Hotel del Coronado is also less than ten miles from the most visited city in the world. Once considered a dusty, sailor's bar-hopping retreat, Tijuana today is Mexico's fourth largest city with a population of more than 1.3 million (second only to Los Angeles along the North American Pacific Coast). More than 42 million people cross the international border between San Diego and Tijuana each year. Going to Tijuana is one of the most popular day trips of hotel guests. They go for the shopping bargains of leather goods, pottery, jewelry and clothing, and also because of the growing number of fine restaurants offering international cuisines.

CONVENTIONS Over the past several years, the Hotel del Coronado has become known as one of the West's great meeting and convention facilities. Hundreds of groups, both large and small, take advantage of the hotel's complete list of services. The Del has thirty meeting and banquet rooms which accommodate from twenty-five to 1500 people. The Grand Hall convention center can be subdivided into three individual soundproof rooms, each holding up to 500 persons: Regent, Empress and Oxford Halls. Other large meeting rooms include the International Room, directly below the Grand Ballroom (400 persons), and the magnificent Crown Room, which can accommodate up to 1000 people for group dining.